CAREERS FOR

WRITERS

& Others Who Have a Way with Words

CAREERS

FOR

WRITERS

& Others Who Have a Way with Words

Robert W. Bly

VGM Career Horizons

NTC/Contemporary Publishing Group

Library of Congress Cataloging-in-Publication Data

Bly, Robert.
    Careers for writers & others who have a way with words / Robert Bly.
       p.   cm.—(VGM careers for you series)
    Includes bibliographical references.
    ISBN 0-8442-4333-7 (cloth)
    ISBN 0-8442-4334-5 (paper)
    1. Authorship—Vocational guidance.   I. Title.   II. Series.
  PN151.B62   1996
  808'.02—dc20   95-23253
                                                    CIP

Published by VGM Career Horizons
A division of NTC/Contemporary Publishing Group, Inc.
4255 West Touhy Avenue, Lincolnwood (Chicago), Illinois 60646-1975 U.S.A.
Copyright © 1996 by NTC/Contemporary Publishing Group, Inc.
All rights reserved. No part of this book may be reproduced, stored in a retrieval
system, or transmitted in any form or by any means, electronic, mechanical,
photocopying, recording, or otherwise, without the prior written permission of
NTC/Contemporary Publishing Group, Inc.
Printed in the United States of America
International Standard Book Number: 0-8442-4333-7 (cloth)
                                       0-8442-4334-5 (paper)
99 00 01 02 03 04 VP 21 20 19 18 17 16 15 14 13 12 11 10 9 8 7 6 5 4

Contents

About the Author

B ob Bly is a full-time free-lance writer specializing in business-to-business, high-tech, and direct marketing. Bob is the author of thirty-five books including *Creative Careers: Real Jobs in Glamour Fields* (John Wiley & Sons), *The Elements of Business Writing* (Macmillan), *The Elements of Technical Writing* (Macmillan), *The Copywriter's Handbook* (Henry Holt & Co.), and *Secrets of a Freelance Writer* (Henry Holt & Co.). Thousands of writers have attended his popular seminars, "How to Write a Nonfiction Book and Get It Published" and "How to Make $85,000+ a Year as a Freelance Writer."

Mr. Bly's articles have appeared in such publications as *Amtrak Express, Computer Decisions, Cosmopolitan, New Jersey Monthly,* and *Writer's Digest.* He has been a featured speaker at writers' conferences nationwide.

Mr. Bly has held a number of writing-related jobs. He was a technical writer for Westinghouse Electric Corporation and a communications manager for Koch Engineering. As a freelancer, he has handled writing assignments for more than one hundred clients, including AT&T, IBM, ITT, Medical Economics, Reed Travel Group, Leviton Manufacturing, Associated Air Freight, and Chemical Bank.

Acknowledgments

The author would like to thank the following people for providing information about their careers:

Eve Blake
Gary Blake
David Dwek
Charles Flowers
Don Hauptman
Linda Ketchum
David Kohn
Paul Karasik
Milt Pierce
Tom Quirk
Julie and Dave Schroeder
Terry Smith
Amy Sprecher Bly
Robert Varitoni
Joe Vitale
Craig Wolf

The section "Estimating a Technical Writing Job" in Chapter 8 is a slightly modified version of text appearing in John Lancaster's book, "How to Make Money Writing Technical Manuals" (self-published). Reprinted with permission.

This book is for Joe Vitale, a writer's writer.

Foreword

I didn't become a writer by intent. Unlike a doctor or a dentist, my career path didn't follow any sort of plan. Rather, things just happened, and I went with the flow.

Would I recommend this to you? It has its pros and cons. I have had many delightful surprises, twists, and turns I might not have experienced had I followed the straight and narrow path. These include having many books published on a variety of interesting subjects, being a guest on television and radio shows, and getting nice checks for free-lance assignments. People are fascinated with writers, and if you are one or become one, many will seek your advice on how they too can get published.

On the other hand, planning a deliberate career has its advantages, too. When you become more knowledgeable about a job or industry, your chances of getting the job you want are improved. And you will probably earn more, sooner.

This book contains a wealth of information on numerous writing careers—both staff and free-lance—in literature, journalism, and commercial writing.

How am I qualified to guide you? I have been a writer since I graduated college in 1979. I spent three years in the corporate world and have thirteen years' experience free-lancing for newspapers, magazines, book publishers, and corporate clients.

I am not the most prolific writer in the world, but I am not a slacker. I have one hundred articles and twenty-eight books published, with seven more books under contract or on press. I wrote my first book in 1982 and since have averaged two to three books a year.

During this time, I have earned the bulk of my income doing free-lance writing for corporate clients. Assignments include brochures, direct mail packages, ads, sales letters, press releases, and manuals. I am not rich on the Stephen King/Danielle Steele level, but I make a decent living, having earned more than a million dollars in fees and royalties from my free-lance writing since I started in February 1982.

I tell you this not to brag, but to let you know this book is based on years of real-life experience making a living as a writer. It's long on practical how-to advice and short on theory.

Science fiction writer Roger Zelazny has said that he loves being a writer, even the paperwork. I don't like the paperwork, but other than that, I agree with Roger: The writing life is a great life. Since writing often doesn't pay well compared with other professions, you shouldn't go into writing unless you love to write. If you do, this book is for you.

CHAPTER ONE

The Writing Business

My Own Story

Writing is an intensely personal act. Even when you're doing commercial work for an employer or client, you put a lot of yourself in your writing. So it's appropriate that I begin this book on making money as a writer with the story of how I got into the writing business. It will help you to see how writers end up becoming writers in real life. And maybe you can learn from my mistakes.

I didn't set out to be a writer. My earliest ambition was to be a pediatrician because I like children. In junior high, I enjoyed debating and thought I might become a lawyer.

In high school, my favorite subjects were chemistry, biology, and physics, and I decided I wanted to be a scientist.

I love books and always have. Throughout school I was a voracious reader. Ms. Shern, our sixth grade teacher, gave sweets as prizes to students who read the most books each week. I was a constant winner and therefore a slightly overweight eleven-year-old.

I didn't read all those books to win raspberry tarts, however. I just loved to read. And still do. I am a book person, "bookish," a book worm.

Yet it never occurred to me to be a writer. Writers, to me, were artists starving in garrets. As a level-headed boy from a middle-class family in Fair Lawn, New Jersey, I favored going into a "real" profession—medicine, law, science, engineering.

In 1975, I graduated high school and began my freshman year at the University of Rochester. My major was chemistry. I was set to become a research scientist.

But a funny thing happened. As I moved from the introductory to the advanced courses, my ability to see concepts, solve problems, and understand the material began to falter. I soon saw that I did not have the type of brain that would make for a successful scientist. I enjoyed the basics, but the complexities were beyond my grasp. I would always love science, but as a layperson, not a professional. I tell people today that my understanding of science is limited to how Carl Sagan presents it, and no further.

But there I was, now a sophomore and without a clear career direction. Since I did not want to throw three semesters of science and math courses down the drain, I did something really stupid. I switched, without really understanding what I was doing, into the major most closely related to chemistry: chemical engineering.

I was mediocre at chemistry, but positively awful at chemical engineering. I had trouble with the mathematical problem solving and was inept at laboratory work. Worse, I was now "stuck" in a major aiming me toward a career for which I had no aptitude and little interest. My parents were unaware of my aimlessness or that I had gone so far off the track.

But two events happened around this time that ultimately set the direction for the rest of my working life.

The first is that I noticed I had an aptitude for writing. In our labs, we worked as a team: one student performed the experiment; one did the calculations and the graphs; the third wrote the report. I found the report writing was the only part of this I was good at and enjoyed. My instructors complimented my writing even as they criticized my ineptness at handling equipment. One in particular often engaged me in discussions of wording and style; I remember a long debate about the acceptability of beginning a sentence with the word "however." (He was against it. I was in favor of it. However, that's another story....)

Based on this newfound interest, I tried writing short stories and got several published in the student literary magazine. One even got accepted by *Galaxy*, a science fiction magazine. But the magazine went out of business; I was never paid and the story was never published.

The second event happened in the school cafeteria, where I worked washing dishes The editor of the school paper came up to me and said, "I liked your stories in the literary magazine. Why don't you try writing for the school paper?"

I showed up the next day at the school paper offices, and that's where my real college education started. Although we were a small school, the newspaper was published daily, and there began my intensive training in writing.

Seeing my by-line in the school newspaper and magazine, and getting recognition from fellow students, thrilled me beyond anything that had happened to me until that time. I wasn't an athlete in high school, so never got the recognition and kudos many teenage boys do. But in writing, and getting my writing published, I found my identity, my calling, my satisfaction. I was hooked.

I began spending more and more time writing for the daily newspaper, less and less time at my chemical engineering studies. My grades slipped from dean's list to warning list, but I didn't care: I knew my vocational training was taking place at the newspaper, not in the classroom. Several science and engineering professors allowed me to write long papers to satisfy class requirements, and I thought I might become a science writer. That would certainly combine my two interests!

In fact, the public relations director of the university's laser fusion research laboratory noticed an article I wrote about the lab's work for the school paper and offered me a summer job as his assistant. However, he had the desire but neither the authority nor the budget to hire me, so nothing came of it. I was crushed. I spent the summer moving boxes in a warehouse.

In my senior year, I had developed a keen interest and some skill in writing. But I have gotten into it by accident; I had no clear career path. Although I had not studied journalism, I thought perhaps I could get a job as a newspaper reporter. My friend, the former editor-in-chief of our school paper, got me an interview with the Associated Press in Buffalo, New York.

Since I didn't have a car, I had to take the bus in the freezing dark on a snowy February morning. I was given a battery of tests by the editor. If I passed, I would be a junior reporter in the AP Buffalo Bureau.

Later, over the phone, the editor informed me: "You didn't get the job. Your writing was good, but not the best of those we interviewed. You were a little slow, taking too long to complete the essays; our reporters must be fast. You scored high on the intelligence test, but...you failed the spelling test."

Had I passed, I would have undoubtedly taken the job and enjoyed a career as a newspaper reporter. However, being rejected by the AP and not granted an interview at any other paper, I was to take a different path.

A Job Interview Pans Out

Toward the end of each school year, managers from major corporations seeking to hire engineers come on campus and interview the senior engineering majors. Having failed to get the writing job I wanted, I still needed to earn money to live and pay back my considerable student loans. I signed up for the interviews and decided to work as an engineer.

Here was a third turn of fate that landed me in my current writing career: Almost none of the companies wanted to hire me as an engineer. They saw clearly that I lacked the enthusiasm and knowledge of the subject my classmates had.

During the interview, recruiters asked about extracurricular activities, and I talked energetically of my work on the school newspaper, of which I had become features editor, and school magazine, of which I had become editor-in-chief. One recruiter said to me after an interview, "You know, you sound as if you are not that interested in engineering but really like to write. Our company hires technical writers, and with your combined background in engineering and writing, you sound like you would be good for the job. Would you like to interview with hiring managers at a couple of our plants?"

I was amazed. It had never occurred to me that the same manufacturing companies that were hiring my classmates as engineers would also pay me a salary to be a writer for them. In fact, I didn't really know what a technical writer did. I was soon to find out.

I interviewed at two different Westinghouse facilities. The first, in Pennsylvania, was a factory that made nuclear plants. The place was rather drab and industrial-looking. The manager needed to add another person to a group of technical writers who wrote instruction manuals for nuclear power plants the company built. He said, "I have to warn you; these manuals are pretty dry stuff. Are you sure this is what you want to do with your life?"

I went into the room where the technical writers worked. Each sat at a desk writing in longhand or typing copy. They looked bored and I'm sure were. It was hot and musty, and you couldn't see out the windows, which were high up the wall.

The manager offered me the job at a salary of $18,500, which was pretty good for 1979 and almost as much as I would have made as an engineer (most of my classmates were starting at $20,000; by comparison, chemical engineers start today at around $40,000). But I didn't take it. Aside from the boredom factor, I noticed that all employees wore special badges to measure the amount of radiation they were exposed to daily. While I was assured that the levels were safe, the fact that my radiation exposure would be monitored was a turn-off. I turned the job down.

My second interview was at the Westinghouse Defense Center in Baltimore, Maryland. The area was suburban and clean, the facility modern and cheery.

The manager who interviewed me, Terry C. Smith, seemed enthusiastic, creative, and happy in his work. Terry was interested in my writing and asked to see my articles from the school paper. After I showed him my clippings, Terry told me that he had written a book, a copy of which he proudly pulled off his bookshelf to show me. Its title was *How to Write Better and Faster*, and it was published in hardcover by Thomas Crowel. I was in the presence of a real author—and duly impressed!

I felt I wanted to work for Terry Smith. He had written a book about writing and could teach me a lot. Also, the writing I would be doing, while technical, seemed more interesting than the nuclear power plant manuals. Terry's department, marketing communications, produced brochures, trade show displays, videotapes, and other promotions used in the marketing of Westinghouse's weapons and defense systems. In contrast to the drab nuclear manual, Terry's group produced colorful, attractive brochures, sell sheets, and ads.

Terry offered me a job at $16,000. I felt this was too low, given what I could earn as an engineer. In between the Westinghouse interviews, I had my one successful interview for an engineering position, and was offered a job as a quality engineer with IBM in up-state New York for $20,000. I told Terry of my other offers, and said I could not take the job for less than $18,500. He offered me $18,500 on the spot, and I immediately accepted. And that's how I got my first paying job as a writer.

After less than a year with Westinghouse, Mike Mutsakis, a product manager with Koch Engineering, a manufacturer of chemical equipment, called. Mike had also offered me a job out of college, but I felt I could learn more from Terry, and went with Westinghouse. Mike had never filled the position and was convinced I was the right person—apparently, he had difficulty finding writers with chemical engineering degrees. Mike flew me to New York City for an interview and offered me $27,000 plus perks I didn't have at Westinghouse, such as a private office. I also liked the idea of moving to Manhattan. I accepted.

In addition to writing brochures and technical papers, at Koch I was responsible for administering the company's advertising and trade show activities. I liked Koch Engineering, but began to grow bored and dissatisfied for a number of reasons. When the new company president asked me to move to the manufacturing headquarters in Wichita, Kansas, I decided to resign and try free-lancing.

My parents thought I was nuts to give up a high-paying corporate job for the uncertainties of free-lancing. And maybe they were right. But I was young, single, without financial responsibilities. Although not a risk taker by nature, I went for it and began to promote myself as a free-lance copywriter and technical writer in February 1982.

The first year, I earned $38,000 in gross income—more than my engineering firm salary, which had risen to $29,500. However, Manhattan has an astronomical cost of living, and so I lived very modestly. I didn't own a car, and I lived and worked in a one-room studio apartment.

By the way, the best financial advice I ever heard for writers comes from Florida editor David Kohn, who says, "Live below your means." As a writer, you may enjoy a handsome income, or your earnings may be modest. If your overhead is low, you can live nicely on a lower income and not feel constantly pressured to earn more.

The next year I made over $50,000; then over $80,000 the third year. After that, I was delighted and surprised that I always grossed well in excess of $100,000 a year. Through a series of happy accidents, I had become a full-time free-lance writer, earning my living exclusively through my writing.

Why Do You Want to Be a Writer?

I became a free-lance writer largely by accident. Should you or anyone do it on purpose?

We'll discuss the pros and cons shortly. But let me tell you this: If money is your primary goal, and you want to become wealthy, writing is not the career choice I would recommend to you.

Many writers see the kind of money that best-selling authors and Hollywood screenwriters make and think they can duplicate that success. It's possible, but a long shot. Only a small percentage of writers make six- and seven-figure incomes. Most have modest incomes. And only a handful become famous. Most live in relative obscurity.

Writing is not a sure path to the lifestyles of the rich and famous. In fact, several surveys have pegged the average annual income of full-time writers in the United States at just $25,000.

The main reason to become a writer, in my opinion, is writing is what you love to do more than anything else, and the thought of doing something other than writing eight hours a day, five days a week bores you to tears. You may be interested in finance and medicine and travel, but you would rather write about them than be an investment banker, neurologist, or travel agent. I once asked Andy Neff, a financial journalist, why he didn't go to work as a broker or analyst, and instead preferred to be a reporter, which paid well but not as much as these other positions. Replied Andy, "I think it's more fun to watch."

Writers are interested in a diverse range of subjects but prefer to move from field to field to satisfy intellectual curiosity, rather than devote an entire working life to one particular discipline. When I was a technical writer at Westinghouse, I enjoyed learning about the many activities of the company, the many technologies we were developing. But I would never want to spend my whole day, never mind my whole career, working on just one of them. One engineer I interviewed had spent ten years working on the antenna configuration for one particular model of a radar system we manufactured. This topic held my interest while I wrote an article on it for the company magazine, but I never wanted to have a job that narrow and confining. You probably feel the same way.

So again: The main reason to become a writer is because you love to write, and you want to spend your days doing it and getting paid for it.

To make writing a career, the compulsion to write should be strong within you. If the urge to write is mild—that is, if writing is an interest rather than a passion or an addiction—you need not make it your career to satisfy your urge: You can write poems during your lunch hour, short stories at night, work on your novel during the weekend. You can submit articles and essays to magazines, get published, get paid, and see your byline in print. You can even write books and become a bona fide author without making it your full-time job. You can attend writers' conferences, read writers' magazines, join writers' clubs, and lead a literary life in your spare hours, after your regular job.

But for those of us who become full-time writers, writing in our spare time evenings and weekends isn't enough to satisfy the writing urge. We feel unfulfilled, bored, and discontented when we work at jobs that are other than writing. We don't want to spend our days attending meetings, managing projects, supervising employees, or doing other non-writing tasks. We want to write and do writing-related chores like research, interviews, and reading. So although we may be able to make more money in other positions or careers, we choose instead to be writers.

Most writers I know are introverts, and most are not "people persons." I don't mean to say that writers dislike people. I mean that given the choice between spending the day all alone in a room in front of a word processor or being in the more social environment of the conventional workplace, writers usually choose the solitude of writing. Writer Fran Liebowitz says, "I do not work well with others, nor do I wish to learn how to do so."

Many writers, but not all, are curmudgeons. We do not quite fit into the social mainstream, and often feel out of place in a corporate setting. Technical writer Peter Kent said, only half joking, that one reason he chose to become a free-lance technical writer was so he wouldn't have to wear a suit and tie every day.

Certainly, not having to wear a tie is a perk for me. But what about you? There are advantages to the writing life, but also disadvantages. Let's look at the pros and cons so you can make an informed decision about whether to pursue this as your career instead of an avocation or hobby.

Advantages of Being a Writer

There are many advantages to making a career of writing.

YOU GET TO WRITE.   Writers spend a good part of their days, although not all of their days, using words to make sentences. If you like to write, you will be doing work that is relatively pleasant and enjoyable to you. This sets you apart from the large majority of workers who spend their days doing work they do not find enjoyable or fulfilling.

Few people dream of selling tickets at an airline reservation counter, collecting highway tolls, assembling the same machine part a hundred times every day, or buying office and building supplies. Yet thousands of people employed as airline reservation clerks, toll collectors, factory workers, and purchasing agents do these things every day.

Many people, on the other hand, dream of writing and getting published, and as a full-time writer, you can get paid to do both.

YOU GET PUBLISHED. Writer May Sarton once observed that while many people want to hold a book with their name on the cover, many of them don't actually want to do the hard part and write the book. For some people, the glory and excitement is in getting published and seeing your work in print.

Writing is unusual in that many writers get to sign their name to their work. Factory workers don't sign their names to cars they helped build, and surgeons don't sign their names on patients on whom they operated. Writers, however, get a lot of public credit for their work. Script writers see their names in the credits of movies and television shows. Authors see their names on book covers. Journalists have by-lines in magazines and newspapers.

Some writers—technical writers, advertising copywriters, and public relations writers, to name a few—do not get by-lines. But they still get enormous pleasure from seeing their work in print. I was never as thrilled in my writing career as when the first brochure I had written at Westinghouse was printed. Although I received no by-line or credit, it gave me enormous satisfaction to hold copies of that beautiful color brochure in which my words were so attractively printed to accompany the many photos and illustrations.

Even when you don't get a by-line, your writing produces tangible results you can hold in your hand, show to others, and keep permanently: Newsletters, press releases, brochures, ads, videos, articles can all be clipped and saved and shown to friends and colleagues. In many professions, people retain no tangible evidence of their work. A purchasing agent, for example, does not keep the products she purchases for her company. A tailor does not keep the suits he sews. But if you write an article for an editor or a booklet for a client, you can get copies and show them off as your work. This is a nice perk not available with many other professions.

Aside from the personal satisfaction, keeping and sharing copies of your work helps promote your career, whether you are seeking a promotion, a job with a new company, or free-lance writing assignments. Therefore, writers are not as dependent on good references and recommendations as other workers because they can bring samples of their work to job interviews and show them to potential employers and clients.

Writers, unlike most other professionals, are judged more by the work they have done than by what others say about them. So if your writing is good, you can get work. Yes, it's important to get along with and please people. But you are not wholly dependent on what others say about you when it comes to getting hired.

YOU CAN SOMETIMES MAKE VERY GOOD MONEY.   Writing is not a "monied" profession. Writers, on average, earn much less than accountants, orthodontists, dentists, attorneys, management consultants, stock brokers, financial planners, doctors, airline pilots, executives, and other professionals. Many full-time writers have a spouse or significant other who earns more money, allowing them the freedom to be writers and earn less. Many other writers remain childless and even single, so they do not have to earn large sums to live comfortably. Some even sacrifice creature comforts in pursuit of their art. I remember reading an interview with John Calvin Batchelor, the novelist, which described his tiny, minimally furnished New York City apartment. Since then, of course, he has had enormous success and, I am sure, lives quite nicely.

Yet although writing is not a high-paying profession, there are some writers who make a lot of money and others who periodically make big money from writing projects. At the top of the money tree are the best-selling novelists and big-name Hollywood screenwriters, who command seven-figure advances and fees.

But you don't have to be a best-selling novelist or famous Hollywood writer to make big money writing. Jim Reutz, for example, earns more than a million dollars a year as a writer, yet you have never heard of him. That's because Jim writes direct-mail promotions for newsletter publishers and other direct marketers for whom winning copy means the difference between success and failure. They pay Jim handsome royalties on direct mail packages that are sometimes mailed in quantities of one million pieces or more.

Big money can be made by writers in other fields, as well. Although the average journalist earns about $33,000 a year, some earn close to seven figures. A recent article about *New York Post* gossip columnist Liz Smith, for example, hinted that her annual compensation was close to a million dollars. The top sports writers and financial journalists in the country also earn $200,000 to $300,000 a year or more writing articles or syndicated columns for major newspapers and magazines.

And there are other avenues for making big money as a writer. Jeffrey Lant, a writer in Cambridge, Massachusetts, has become a millionaire by writing, self-publishing, and selling books, special reports, and other information products. Dan Poynter, a writer in Santa Barbara, California, has earned millions of dollars by writing, self-publishing, and selling books on parachuting and other sports.

You don't have to be a "creative" writer to make a fortune. Stephanie Winston is an author who writes on a topic many would consider mundane: how to become more organized in your work and at home. She has written only two books on this topic, yet these books in all editions have sold more than 1.6 million copies, making Stephanie a wealthy woman. She attended a writing workshop I gave in New York City, and I was thrilled to hear of her success.

While many writing jobs pay poorly, some pay extremely well. Corporate speech writers and communications managers often earn salaries of $70,000 to $100,000 a year or even more, plus a lot of benefits.

YOU HAVE FLEXIBLE HOURS. Free-lance writers can set their own hours. In many ad agencies, writers can work hours other than nine to five, as long as they put in the time. Contract technical writers can sometimes negotiate to do some of the work at home, if they have computer systems compatible with what the employer uses at work, and can therefore also have more flexibility in their schedules. Book writers especially have great freedom: They are given a deadline, and from the time they get the book contract to when they hand in the book, they are relatively free to do what they please, come and go when they please. It's a very nice life.

To me, this is one of the major perks. Actually, I work during normal work hours, so I am available to my clients during the day and am free to spend time with my young sons evenings and weekends. Many writers I know tend to be nocturnal; they are late risers who prefer to sleep in and then work late in the evening.

Because my office is two miles from my home, my commute is short, so unlike my corporate counterparts, I do not have to get up early in the morning—something I always had trouble with and disliked. I do not use an alarm clock and am awakened each morning between 7:30 and 8:30 A.M. by my kids, which is just fine with me. If they get up late, I can always stay a little later to play with them before going to the office; I do not punch a time clock, nor am I accountable to a boss for my whereabouts.

YOU CAN WEAR INFORMAL ATTIRE. Unless they are seeing clients or editors, free-lance writers can dress however they want. Ad agency and PR writers are often in environments where casual dress is acceptable. Most writers employed by corporations, however, must dress in conventional business clothes.

It's a great advantage to wear what you want to. For one thing, I find I work better because I am more comfortable. I save · money on clothes and dry cleaning because I'm in a suit and tie maybe five hours a week at most—and not at all during many weeks. I can also get up later because I need not be clean-shaven, put on a suit, polish my shoes, or have every hair combed neatly into place. I actually think it takes an enormous amount of energy for men, and perhaps more for women, to look presentable at work each day, and I am glad I do not have to go through such tiring and time-consuming rituals each morning.

YOU GAIN FAME. Writers, even those who are not on the best-seller list, get more attention than people in most other professions. By-lines make us highly visible. Even if people have not read your work or heard of you, many become interested and envious when they hear you are a writer.

Most writers gain minor fame only, but even this can be enormously satisfying. Because of my writing, I have lectured to members of large associations and employees of prestigious corporations; been asked for my autograph; received hundreds of fan letters and dozens of nice phone calls and e-mail messages from readers; and appeared as a guest on numerous radio and TV talk shows. This doesn't put bread on the table, but in some ways it can be satisfying.

Even writers like myself who are not famous will have some fans. It is fascinating to realize there are some people who follow what you do and want to read everything you write! If you are a corporate writer, you will become highly visible within the organization because you are always interviewing people for press releases or the company newsletter.

YOU HELP OTHERS. Most writing is designed to entertain, inform, or instruct. Therefore, people either enjoy reading what you write, or they benefit from the information your writing conveys. Either way, you are making life better and more enjoyable for others. That's a nice feeling.

Yes, most of the things we write may be news oriented or commercial in nature, and not have much impact. But every once in a while, an article or book you write changes someone's life for the better ... and they let you know it. I enjoy it most when a reader says, "Your book helped me in my life." That's a powerful reward.

THERE IS A CONSTANT DEMAND FOR YOUR SERVICES.   Writing is a service in universal demand. Practically every individual and organization needs materials written; a large number of these pay staff or free-lance writers to turn out newsletters, articles, bulletins, and announcements on a daily or weekly basis.

Some have predicted that the current high illiteracy rate, combined with the growing popularity of computers and other electronic media, is reducing the need for writing services, and may even make printed reading material obsolete. This is untrue. If anything, the computer age is creating new opportunities for writers. Writers are now getting paid to write CD-ROM presentations, multimedia presentations, even HELP screens for software. And while rising illiteracy rates do reduce the number of readers, keep in mind that our population is growing at a frantic rate. So while a lower percentage of people read, there are more customers overall to buy your work.

YOU ENJOY A CERTAIN FREEDOM AND INDEPENDENCE.   In corporate America, speech writers and other staff writers, while nicely compensated, are somewhat out of the mainstream of the business and corporate world.

You often hear the distinction between *line* and *staff* jobs. People who hold line positions, like product managers and process engineers, do work that is essential to the primary business of the company: A product manager at Cleano Soap literally runs the business for that product line, while a process engineer makes sure the product is produced economically and in required quantities on schedule. Line people become totally involved in the business of the corporation; it is their main concern and the focus of their work life.

People who hold staff jobs do work that, while desired, is not essential to the running of the company. Therefore their identity is usually tied more to what they do and less to what the company does.

On the other hand, writers at Cleano are probably more interested in writing than in Cleano Soap. Computer programmers at Cleano are probably more interested in Cobol and BASIC than in soap. These people derive satisfaction from their craft; their identity is as a writer or programmer, not a Cleano Soap team member. This gives them a certain distance from the mainstream of corporate America and independence that many enjoy and embrace. It lets them be a little bit of a rebel even within their mainstream lifestyle. And we all have a little bit of the rebel within us.

THERE ARE TAX ADVANTAGES. Many writers—full-time freelancers as well as those corporate employs who moonlight—enjoy significant tax deductions not available to the average working person. They can deduct all or part of the cost of their computer, software, computer paper, floppy disks, and other office supplies. They may also get deductions for postage, telephone bills, and having space at home which they use as an office. But be sure to consult with your accountant as to what is deductible for you and what is not. Otherwise you could get in trouble and owe the Internal Revenue Service a lot of money.

Disadvantages of Being a Full-Time Writer

YOU ARE TOLD WHAT TO WRITE. Many writers don't always write what they want. Subject, length, and even tone and style are frequently dictated by a client, editor, or employer.

For instance, this week, I am writing a brochure about a wiring system used in constructing buildings so they can accommodate workstations, PCs, and other data communications devices. Is this interesting to me? Yes. Is this what I would write about if I were not getting paid by this client? No.

Writers who make a career of writing usually have to compromise: They get the blessing of avoiding other work and doing just writing in exchange for having to write what the boss or editor wants rather than what the writer wants.

If you want to write only pieces of your own choosing, you would be better off taking a day job doing some other work, then pursuing writing as an avocation nights and weekends. This way you can do as you please without suffering economically. You may even create an original work that makes a lot of money.

This is what happened to Tom Clancy, author of *The Hunt for Red October* and other novels involving espionage, the military, and defense. He was an insurance agent during the day, writing novels in his spare time.

At first, Clancy could not sell his books to mainstream publishers. A small press published his first novel, which became a best-seller and paved the way for a career change from insurance agent to best-selling novelist.

YOUR CREATIVITY IS REIGNED IN.   Creative writing is a form of self-expression. Journalism, technical writing, and advertising copywriting are not. As a corporate writer or journalist, you are communicating a message or delivering news. The content of what you write is shaped by the facts of the story, the client's or editor's preferences, and the objective of the piece.

Many writers feel this type of work is constraining and uncreative. Others feel it is too formula, crass, or commercial. I suggest you try it before you decide how you feel about it.

On the surface, the type of writing jobs described in this book may seem unglamorous. But I have held many of them and found them to be deeply satisfying. The satisfaction is not in creating a piece of writing that is in itself "creative," but in using your creativity to fashion a piece of writing that meets the client's specifications, yet is finely crafted and a delight to read.

YOU MAY NOT MAKE A LOT OF MONEY. Writers' incomes vary widely, and this book goes into specific detail about what you can expect to earn in the various writing careers.

But up front, I want to warn you that writing is not a high-income profession. Some writers are wealthy; many earn handsome salaries; but the *average* annual income for writers is relatively low compared with many other professions.

A recent article in the *Wall Street Journal* stated that the average income of those who listed their profession as "writer" in their income tax returns was $25,000. A survey among members of the American Society of Journalists and Authors showed the average annual income of members who are full-time writers to be $25,000. The average staff journalist earns a little more, $32,000 annually.

Entry-level jobs pay particularly poorly. As I scan various forums for writers on America Online and CompuServe, I see many entry-level positions for writers where the salary ranges from the high teens to low twenties. And this is in the 1990s! My starting salary as a technical writer at Westinghouse was $18,500 in 1979—more than fifteen years ago. So writing salaries have not kept up with inflation.

There are some bright spots. One young writer corresponding on the on-line forums reported that he was earning $50,000 at an ad agency as a copywriter, and he was practically just out of college. Although this is unusual, you do see many help-wanted ads offering writers respectable salaries of $40,000 to $80,000 a year or more. Some corporate speech writers earn incomes in the low six figures.

YOU CAN DEVELOP A POVERTY MENTALITY. Because of a combination of low pay scales, a competitive marketplace, and the strong desire to write and get published, many writers have what I call a "poverty mind-set." This means they do not expect to earn a lot of money, view getting published as more important than the money paid for the publication, and even look down on lucrative writing as commercial hack work.

The problem with the poverty mind-set is that it limits your earnings: If you believe you shouldn't earn a lot of money, you probably won't. So many writers will accept ridiculously low advances, royalties, fees, and salaries simply for the privilege of getting published or getting a writing position.

Don't be afraid to seek a good salary or high fees. Often what writers think of as a lot of money is not. For instance, many writers at my New York seminars think it would be amazing if they could earn $25,000 a year or more as a free-lance writer. I remind them that the salary of the average *doorman* in Manhattan is over $30,000. Certainly writing deserves equal or better compensation as opening a door.

Many writers gasp when I tell them that successful free-lancers charge hourly rates of $50 to $150 or more. "For writing?" they say, awestruck. I remind them that lawyers charge $150 an hour and up, plumbers often charge $40 an hour or more, and even the man who cleans my gutters gets $35 for an hour's work. So $50 an hour or $30,000 a year is not a ridiculous sum to imagine earning. Set your sights higher.

YOU MAY NOT HAVE JOB SECURITY. In the corporate world, there are staff jobs and line jobs. A person with a line job is directly involved in the business of the company, and his or her work contributes directly to the bottom line. Examples include brand managers, vice presidents of manufacturing, and process engineers.

Those with staff jobs are not directly involved in the business of the company; they provide services used by others within the company. Examples include technical writers, computer programmers, purchasing agents, and training directors. Since line people are more directly involved with the business, they are usually considered more important, and their jobs are more secure. As a writer, you have a staff job and are more expendable. When corporations downsize, writers, marketing communications people, and training directors are almost always among the first to be let go.

MANY PEOPLE WILL NOT TREAT YOU RESPECTFULLY. Although some people will be impressed that you are a writer, many people treat writers with disrespect. The primary reason, I think, is that ours is a "soft skill" that most people possess to some degree. That is, practically everyone can write. Not as well as you, the professional writer, but well enough to put together a sentence, paragraph, or even a letter, article, report, or talk.

A large number of people feel writing is not a specialized skill, that there is no mystery to what writers do; therefore, writing is a lower-level profession. (Many others, incidentally, greatly admire skill in writing and admit they have little such skill themselves.)

Those who have a specific technical skill, such as x-ray technicians, diesel mechanics, chemical engineers, CPAs, investment bankers, attorneys, and systems analysts, command more respect because others cannot do what they do. Or, if they do not command respect, people are less likely to criticize and question their work simply because of its technical, specialized nature.

At times, however, it may seem as if everybody is a writer, and everybody is telling you how to write the piece. This is one of the hazards of the profession. All you can do is get used to it and tolerate it with a smile.

YOU WILL BE DEPENDENT ON MASTERY OF A SOFT SKILL. Because writing is a soft skill, you may suffer from some anxiety and uncertainty. Many of us who earn our living through soft skills—writers, speakers, trainers, consultants, entrepreneurs—secretly worry that we missed the boat by not having a trade or being qualified to do something more specific and tangible, such as programming AS/400 computers or becoming certified welders.

To some extent, it's true that without a hard skill or trade, you may at times be shut out of jobs in an increasingly technology-oriented marketplace. On the other hand, soft skills are always needed—writers are always needed—but technology can make certain hard skills obsolete. So those whose livelihood depends on a hard skill may in reality have less job security, not more, than us.

YOU FACE HEAVY COMPETITION.   Advertising writer Stan Friedberg once wrote a song called "Everybody Wants to Be an Art Director." Actually, I think he missed the mark, and it should have been, "Everybody Wants to Be a Writer."

At times, it seems as if everybody does want to be a writer. So there is a lot of competition. That's one reason fees are often low—prices are dictated by supply and demand, and the supply of writing sometimes seems to outweigh the demand.

Actually, that's true in literary writing, but not in commercial work. In corporate and marketing writing, there is a lot of competition, but there is even more work, so fees and salaries are higher.

Here's an amazing fact about writing: What you want to do as a living and get paid for, others want to do as a hobby and for free. Writing is a popular avocation. As a result, we professionals must compete with amateurs willing to do our work at slave wages. This is the case in practically no other profession. For example, plumbers don't compete with hobbyists who want to fix people's toilet bowls just for the fun of it. But writers who write for money compete with hobbyists who write just for the fun of it every day.

WRITING IS OFTEN PERCEIVED AS A COMMODITY SERVICE. Because writing is a generic or "soft" skill, writing is often perceived as a commodity service. That is, the employer or client hires or buys mainly on price, not quality or skill. This is not always the case. It's probably not true even in the majority of cases. But beware that there are those who see no difference between a well-published professional or an untried novice; to them, we're just "the writer."

My advice is to work only for employers, clients, and editors who value your skill. Do not work for those who see what you do as a commodity and buy on price.

YOU ARE OUTSIDE THE MAINSTREAM OF CORPORATE AMERICA. Some writers see this as a plus, but you may feel differently. Writers are often viewed in corporate America as odd ducks who somehow are not part of the good-old-boy network. Some writers eventually switch careers, going into management or other areas that are more mainstream.

SOCIETY IS AGAINST YOU. If you decide to free-lance, be aware that society is not oriented to accommodate your lifestyle. As a self-employed writer, you will have more trouble than a corporate worker in qualifying for mortgages and other loans, even though you may be earning more money. Self-employed people are also penalized financially because they must buy their own health insurance. Free-lancers in Canada, of course, are covered at no cost under the national system and don't have this heavy burden.

CHAPTER TWO

Book Publishing

*I*s book publishing glamorous? Many people think of publishing as the brave handmaiden to great books, an industry in which editors goad talented but wayward authors to fashion enduring art. And book publishing does have its moments—the feel of a new hardcover book, the thrill of seeing your book in a bookstore, the editorial satisfaction of unearthing a worthy manuscript, the convivial luncheons, the pungent gossip.

But don't judge a book by its cover. In a *U.S. News and World Report* interview published shortly before his death, publisher Alfred A. Knopf said that "taste in publishing, as in all things, has declined, and that has affected the quality of what is printed. Just look at the fiction and nonfiction best-seller lists. They are full of diets, health, exercise." Knopf went on to say that most editors no longer work closely with authors because there are just too many other things to do. "By the time they get around to publishing one book, they are already working on a new book they have just bought."

There are many other criticisms that one can level at book publishing—that the pay is paltry, that too many books are being published, that too few have any real merit, that the conglomerates have made publishing just another business—but somehow, each generation, legions of book lovers compete to become editors.

From cave walls to computer terminals, writing has been a tool for recording human knowledge, history, and dreams. And no matter how far the computer takes us, there will probably always be people for whom a book is something wonderful and irreplaceable.

Although our discussion of book publishing will focus on editorial work—especially the editing of adult trade books—we acknowledge that there can be a great deal of glamour in publicity and advertising positions as well. By breaking into advertising and publicity in this field, writers can work with books and authors, aiming toward more responsibility and good pay and using many of the same types of interpersonal skills needed for success in editing.

Marketing and Promotion

Of the more than seventy thousand people in book publishing, only about 15 percent do editorial work; 25 percent work in marketing. (The others do everything else, including administration, sales, and distribution.) Here's a brief summary of some of the key marketing positions that involve writing as part of the job.

PUBLICITY DIRECTOR (salary range: $30,000–$50,000). A publicity director is responsible for publicizing all books on a publisher's seasonal list. According to Cynthia Kirk, director of publicity and promotion at Donald I. Fine Inc., to do the job well, you need "a high level of energy and curiosity. You have to be interested in books and be familiar with media. You have to have the flexibility to say to yourself, 'If approach A doesn't work, I'll try approach B.' "

The glamorous part of the job is working with authors, some of whom are well known. Lining up an author for "The CBS Morning News" or the "Tonight" show is a high. Publicity directors arrange book tours, supervise the writing of promotional material, and coordinate the publisher's overall efforts at promoting books and authors.

PUBLICIST (salary range: $18,000–$35,000).   A publicist does many of the things that a publicity director does, but he or she usually works with less famous authors. Publicists usually write their own press releases and are responsible for promoting a certain number of the publisher's books. These people are instrumental in helping authors get television and radio appearances and, in some cases, helping them plan tours of different cities to promote their books. They may also help plan publication parties and events aimed at spotlighting the news angles of certain books. A *publicity assistant*, a lower-level position usually paying $15,000–$25,000, helps the publicist follow through on promotional ideas, which can involve everything from mailing review copies (books sent to the media) to distributing press releases. Generally, strong writing ability, good interpersonal skills, and a head for details are the publicist's key tools on the job.

ADVERTISING DIRECTOR (salary range: $35,000–$65,000). This person helps create and place advertisements for the publisher's books. He or she must be familiar with the media in order to find the best "mix" of advertising—the right magazines, the right newspapers, the best television programs in which to advertise a particular book. Working with sales, marketing, and editorial staffs, the advertising director tries to divide attention among all the publisher's books. Realistically, though, only a handful of books get the advertising director's full attention. Before becoming an advertising director, you may start as a copywriter.

COPYWRITER (salary range: $17,000–$40,000).   Copywriters, sometimes also known as *advertising assistants*, write the advertising copy that helps sell books. This copy may be print advertising, the description of a book on its jacket (known as *flap copy*), or fliers. The job tests your abilities to put yourself into the world of a variety of books, usually about a variety of subjects. It's a delight to see an advertisement you've created appear in the *New York Times Book Review*, for instance.

MARKETING DIRECTOR (salary range: $40,000–$85,000). The marketing director takes overall responsibility for marketing efforts. He or she usually supervises ten to twenty people, including the *ad director* and the *promotion director*.

These positions exist at almost every publishing house and are generally considered essential. In fact, some editors complain that sales and marketing people have more influence than they do when it comes to deciding which books to buy.

It is not hard for publicity assistants to work their way up to higher positions. After finishing their daily chores, ambitious souls can always volunteer to write a press release, to book an author on a radio show, or to put together a list of television stations that should receive a copy of an upcoming book. The road from publicity assistant to publicist to publicity director to director of publicity and advertising has been traveled many times. In this field, it is not uncommon to switch companies frequently in search of more responsibility, more money, and a better title.

Many of the same personnel agencies, reference books, and publishing programs we mention later in this chapter can be of help to the fledgling advertising or publicity assistant. Before a book can be published, however, it must first be edited. No wonder many people equate the editor with the entire publishing process.

Book Editing

In publishing, there are many editors, but few actually edit books that are written by publishing's superstars. The glamorous side of publishing is working at one of a dozen or so top publishing houses, editing the cream of the manuscripts that are submitted for publication, and working with writers, agents, book reviewers, and book clubs to ease the passage of a book from conception to publication to public acceptance.

The glamour of publishing is built, in part, on its legendary figures: Bennett Cerf, the colorful founder of Random House; Alfred A. Knopf, outspoken pioneer and founder of Knopf; Max Perkins, editor to Hemingway, Fitzgerald, and Wolfe; Ken McCormick, former editor-in-chief of Doubleday; Michael Korda, flamboyant editor of Simon and Schuster. At the moment, Korda may be publishing's most notable symbol of success and glamour. On June 3, 1984, Simon and Schuster had seven books on the *New York Times* best-seller list. Among this company's best-selling authors are Clive Cussler (*Raise The Titanic!*), Harold Robbins (*The Carpetbaggers*), Joan Didion (*Democracy*), and New York City's Mayor Ed Koch (*Mayor*).

There's nothing wrong with aspiring to that kind of heady success, but first you have to be realistic about what publishing is and what it is not.

It is not a place for writers or English majors who simply "like books." Editors edit and publish books but generally do not write them. So don't think that publishing is the place to be while you grind out novels at night. Publishing is a business. Recently, many independent publishers have merged with or been acquired by larger companies, making them more accountable to accountants and top management than to literary ideals. Fewer and fewer commercially risky books are being published. These days, a large number of publishable books tend to be "safe bets," and one of publishing's most charming facets—the occasional risk of publishing a worthy manuscript by an unknown author—is quickly evaporating. Publishing is also not a place for people who dream of great wealth. Salaries have always been low. And even at these salaries, you're more likely to be fired for not producing in this field than you would be in a similar position in the corporate world. Samuel Vaughan, editor-in-chief of Doubleday, once listed some of the prerequisites he felt were necessary for success in publishing. He felt you had to be:

- passionately persuaded about print and committed to the power of the word

- in love with both the idea of books and the ideas in books

- in love with language

- capable of enduring frustration

- possessing "a taste for long odds"

When Vaughan conducts job interviews, he looks for a person with "brains, talent, judgment, energy, taste, flair, courage, and conviction—the sort of puzzling person who appreciates literature but is no snob, who can discover a new genius but can also respect books published for reasons of entertainment."

The book-publishing industry employs only about seventy thousand people (not including booksellers, book manufacturers, or other book-service employees). Only about 1 percent of those have the type of editorial positions at major publishing companies that could be considered "glamorous." There are about twenty-five hundred consistently active book publishers in the United States, but five companies have half of all paperback sales, and the top ten have 86 percent of the market. Roughly fifty thousand books are published each year, and only a small percentage of them ever receive attention in the press.

According to *Publisher's Weekly*, publishing's major trade magazine, industry leaders are bullish on publishing's growth over the next ten years. The greatest growth is occurring in trade (bookstore) books and mass-market paperbacks ("pocket"-size books distributed to supermarkets and other retail outlets in addition to bookstores). Some industry leaders have predicted that the trend toward "brand-name" authors will continue and that the computer will play an increasingly important role in the production, editing, and distribution of books.

Few would-be editors will reach the pinnacle of publishing. Few will get to edit the books of John Updike, Robert Ludlum, Erma Bombeck, Norman Mailer, or Isaac Asimov. Few will have their own tables at 21 or Four Seasons; few will chitchat with author Tom Wolfe or publisher Bob Gottlieb or superagent Swifty Lazar. Only a handful of America's trade editors will ever know the satisfaction of seeing their authors on "The Phil Donahue Show," "The Today Show," or the best-seller list. Maybe only one in five hundred editors will have tête-à-têtes with publishing superstars at the American Booksellers Association Convention cocktail parties or return the nods of colleagues as they stroll through the Frankfurt Book Fair, looking for European best-sellers to buy and publish in the United States.

But being even a small part of an industry in which these things happen is enough for some: the chance to help bring books to life. Here's what editorial assistant Sue Shapiro advises would-be editors:

"I suggest that job-seekers comb *LMP [Literary Market Place]*. Large houses [e.g., Macmillan Publishing] usually have openings. Go to a house that publishes the type of book you like to read. For example, if you like serious fiction or nonfiction, try for Houghton Mifflin, Harper & Row, or Atheneum. Or try FSG [Farrar, Straus and Giroux] or Little, Brown."

Sue also talked about the negative side of editing: "It isn't a literary picnic. There are things you do that are foolish—like the incessant meetings in which nothing gets done. The joke in publishing is that if you don't find anyone to meet with, shut the door and hold a meeting with yourself."

Where can you find a comprehensive list of major American publishers—complete with addresses, telephone numbers, and the publishing house's top personnel? *Literary Market Place*, as Sue suggests, is the place to look. Known as *LMP*, this annual directory is used extensively by people in the book trade as well as by savvy job seekers. It's available at most large libraries and will show you the diversity of jobs available in the field while providing profiles of hundreds of publishing houses.

Publisher's Weekly includes a section called "Weekly Exchange," where job seekers and employers advertise. You won't find prestigious trade publishers advertising for senior editors in this section because those jobs are rarities, but you will find a lot of jobs that offer experience and a chance to get your feet wet.

As you study *PW* and *LMP*, you may be bewildered by the variety of managerial titles, and you may be unable to decide just whom to write to and how to approach a publisher. Do you address a letter to a top editor or to the publisher of the company? Do you start by going to an employment agency? Or do you write to the personnel departments of each house?

Many people start by using an employment agency, but as they gain experience in publishing, they network, use contacts, and apply to decision makers at the publishing houses themselves. When you do gain some experience, you may wish to send a letter to the publisher or president of a company. That person may route your letter to a particular department or editor, but it helps to have the letter filter down from the top.

Training

While many publishing professionals agree that a strong liberal arts background is a helpful prerequisite for editorial work, there's a debate as to the type of vocational training one should have. Many insiders believe that no training program can truly prepare you for the world of books or teach you to uncover the next *Jaws*, *Roots*, or *In Search of Excellence*. Nan Talese, vice-president and executive editor of Houghton Mifflin, wrote in a *Publisher's Weekly* article on publishing careers: "To me, publishing inevitably is more a vocation than a profession. The greatest satisfaction is involvement in the work itself. I doubt there really are any effective training programs; the enormous number of details makes experience in the job the greatest teacher." She goes on to recommend Scott Berg's book, *Maxwell Perkins: Editor of Genius* to show young people both the "daily dross" and the "gold" of publishing.

Most publishers assume that you've had a solid college education. Usually, that means a bachelor's degree in a humanities major, with a varied diet of liberal arts courses, business courses, and even a few computer science courses. Great editors have emerged from a number of disciplines, but it helps to present credentials that show you're well read in literature, economics, marketing, psychology, fine arts, and drama. Any courses you take in art history, graphic design, photography, or printing may also be impressive. Law courses are a big plus, too. And while publishers are not bowled over by advanced academic degrees, they may well take notice of an MBA or an advanced degree in computer science or marketing.

There are several renowned postgraduate courses in publishing, and we'll outline a few of the best. But remember that some publishing executives are skeptical that the skills necessary in the real world of publishing can be learned in a classroom. Many of the top publishers value academic courses as the best training and may well favor a job applicant with an impressive record as an English major over a candidate who lacked the exposure to such an education. The academic courses offered today in publishing will give you a smattering of many important publishing-related skills and experiences, but the best way to "sell" these courses to your interviewer is simply to present them as a "broadening experience" rather than the equivalent of on-the-job training.

Currently, the top three academic publishing programs are offered by Radcliffe, New York University, and the University of Denver. Other excellent programs are available at several dozen colleges and universities throughout the United States.

The Publishing Procedures Course at Radcliffe (10 Garden Street, Cambridge, MA 02138) is an intensive summer professional program for recent college graduates who are seriously considering a career in book publishing. Intended to convey an overall understanding of the requirements and opportunities of publishing, the Radcliffe program provides basic training in publishing skills and brings students into direct contact with publishers. The program has been in existence for more than thirty years.

Allen Peacock worked in the Harvard Co-op textbook department while waiting to get into the Radcliffe program. Today, Peacock, at age twenty-nine, is an editor at Linden Press (a division of Simon and Schuster), with a growing reputation as a fine editor concerned about quality literature and nurturing authors.

The New York University Course (2 University Place, New York, NY 10003), run by the School of Continuing Education, is an intensive four-week program designed to provide a comprehensive overview of book publishing, from initial concept to final sale. Sessions cover acquisition of manuscripts, author–publisher contracts, editing, printing processes, proofreading, copyright, sales promotion, publicity and advertising, and subsidiary rights.

The Publishing Institute at the University of Denver is sponsored by the Graduate School of Librarianship. The Institute offers a concentrated four-week summer program of full-time course work devoted exclusively to book publishing.

There are also excellent courses of study in book publishing at the City University of New York, George Washington University (Washington, D.C.), Hunter College (New York City), Rice University (Houston), Arkansas State University, Hofstra University (Hempstead, New York), Sarah Lawrence College (Bronxville, New York), Simmons College, (Boston), The University of California at Berkeley, and the School of Visual Arts (New York City). City University of New York boasts one of America's most distinguished publishing libraries, the William H. and Gwynn K. Crouse Library for Publishing Arts, located at 33 West Forty-second Street in New York City.

What Editors Do

Acquisitions editors, also sometimes called *senior editors,* buy manuscripts and oversee their publication. They negotiate fees and royalties with agents and writers, attend sales conferences, meet with the publicist assigned to their books, and work with authors, designers, and printers to ensure that the finished book is well written, sound, and attractive. A senior editor with a reputation for talent and sensitivity can be a magnet, attracting top writers of all descriptions. When Ann Harris, for instance, was a senior editor at Harper & Row, she acquired and edited *The Thorn Birds* by Colleen McCullough, *The Times of My Life* by Betty Ford, *The Exorcist* by William Peter Blatty, and *Altered States* by Paddy Chayevsky.

Top editors throw out the formulas; they are on the lookout for creative ways to meet the ever-changing needs of the book-buying public—as when, for instance, Richard Simon and others at Pocket Books proposed to Dr. Benjamin Spock that he write a book about baby care; when Simon and Schuster's financial manager, Leon Shimkin, heard a lecture given by Dale Carnegie and suggested to Mr. Carnegie that his lectures would make a good book (*How to Win Friends and Influence People*, one of the most successful books of all time); and when Sam Vaughan suggested William Buckley, Jr., try his hand at spy novels for Doubleday.

When such editors prove their worth and outgrow their surroundings, they either start their own companies or, in some cases, are given their own imprint within the company—a line of books bearing the editor's name. Richard Marek, who published the early books of Robert Ludlum, has his own imprint, as do Kurt and Helen Wolff, who were responsible for publishing *The Name of the Rose*.

Assistant and *associate editors* do many of the same things that senior editors do, but they generally handle fewer books and less prestigious authors. They also have less say as to what books will be acquired, and they may not be authorized to negotiate fees. In some publishing houses, however, these same titles can be misnomers, actually representing little more than euphemisms for "typist" or "clerk."

Editorial assistant has traditionally translated as glorified secretary, but this will vary from house to house. It's an apprentice position, and you'll probably do a lot of filing, typing, reading manuscripts, and writing reports on the ones you think show promise. If your judgment is keen, you'll be noticed, and usually promoted.

As the low person on the publishing totem pole, you'll probably review manuscripts from the *slush pile*—unsolicited manuscripts from unknown authors. Many editors have started here and have made a reputation by discovering a particularly promising manuscript. *Gone with the Wind* was submitted to Macmillan by an unknown author, and *Ordinary People* was submitted without an agent and became the first unsolicited manuscript Viking had published in a generation. Author William Styron once presided over McGraw-Hill's slush pile—

an autobiographical detail he wove into *Sophie's Choice*—but even Styron failed to spot the potential of an adventure story he found in the pile: *Kon-Tiki*.

The *senior editor* is publishing's glamour-getter, a literary sleuth trying to find publishable books. The *editor-in-chief*—in some houses referred to as the *publisher*—may have a more prestigious title and earn more money, but the job is mainly administrative. As one editor-in-chief put it: "Our job is to produce fifty books out of every two thousand manuscripts we read." Editors-in-chief plan the house's whole publishing program, balancing the season's new titles so that they fulfill the publishing house's general philosophy and marketing aims. They also control the budget and supervise staff.

Working with Authors and Agents

No honest appraisal of the acquisitions editor's job is complete without mentioning that occasionally editors have fierce conflicts with authors. For any of a million reasons, they sometimes slip into adversarial roles as a manuscript undergoes the publishing process. Everyone, of course, wants the book to be a success, but how that success is to be accomplished can be the subject of heated debate. Writers, admittedly, can be unrealistic in their expectations. They can also be perfectionists, or they can be lazy, sloppy, irresponsible, self-centered, reclusive, and even dull.

From the point of view of some writers, a senior editor often looks uncreative, conservative, stingy, unfocused, and glib—little more than an insensitive paper pusher. Writers often can't understand why it takes so long to get a decision from an editor, why advances are so low, why book schedules are so easily thrown out of whack, why editors don't return phone calls. Editors wonder why writers frequently ignore deadlines, ignore author's questionnaires, fight over every single syllable, or insist that an unrealistically large number of copies of their book be printed.

As an editor, you'll need to understand the mind-set of the agent, too. Agents get 10 to 15 percent of what their clients (authors) receive, so they take an assertive, businesslike stance that most authors don't have the time, patience, personality, or experience to take themselves. They'll push you for a decision, tell you that the advance is too low, plead with you to keep the book in print, yell at you because the bookstores aren't stocking the book, and tease you with book ideas that may—if you act immediately—become next year's best-selling titles.

This can be irritating (or amusing), but it's part of the game of publishing, and you may as well get used to it. It can be fun to sit with Scott Meredith over lunch and hear him go on and on about Norman Mailer's new project or Arthur Clarke's latest brainchild. It can be a kick to watch an agent use powers of persuasion to turn a maybe into a yes.

Before too long, you'll know which agents, writers, and colleagues you can trust—and which you can't. Powerhouses like Scott Meredith can boast about the advances (prepublication royalty payment) they've won for their clients (four of the top ten advances ever paid were paid to Meredith's clients: Mailer, Clarke, Carl Sagan, and Margaret Truman). Other agents are more low-key, though they may be just as likely to bring you a marketable manuscript.

Although an editor reads and edits manuscripts, those activities form a surprisingly small part of his or her day. Most of it is spent attending to correspondence, checking galleys and cover designs, talking to agents and authors, meeting with colleagues, and a million and one unglamorous tasks that eat up a workday.

After an editor uncovers a manuscript or book proposal that he or she feels has merit, the editor begins the arduous task of persuading the publisher—and perhaps a board of executives—to buy the book. This may take a few days, a few weeks, or a few months. Agents and authors chew their fingernails while the publishing house ambles toward a decision.

If the answer is no, it's usually final. But if the decision is yes, the editor starts to negotiate for the book. Usually, negotiation entails a few phone conversations with an agent. During these conversations, editor and agent come to an agreement on the specifics of the contract. Among the most important details to be discussed are the amount of the author's advance; the expected date of manuscript submission; the manuscript's anticipated length and date of publication; the ownership of reprint, book-club, serial, and foreign rights; and a number of details involving everything from dramatic rights to royalty percentages to *boilerplate language* (standard clauses) about the author's and publisher's obligations to each other.

This task is not as cumbersome as it sounds. Working your way up as an apprentice, you'll soon become familiar with how contracts are negotiated. Of the many details discussed in each contract, only a handful vary from one book to another.

But the real heart of the job is in taking a manuscript and guiding it through the production process toward becoming a bound book in a store. Roughly speaking, here's what this entails, once the author has submitted an acceptable manuscript:

- Editing the manuscript

- Having the manuscript *copyedited* (closely edited for consistency and style)

- Working with designers and printers to get the book and cover designed (helping to choose a typeface, jacket copy, and cover design)

- Reading and distributing *book galleys* (page proofs of the printed book)

- Working on last-minute changes with author

- Checking and distributing *bound galleys* (proofs bound for distribution to reviewers prior to the actual publication of the finished book)

- Arranging a publicity budget and strategy with the sales force, marketing director, advertising manager, publicity director, and subsidiary-rights director

- Approving the press release

- Inspecting copies of the bound book

Other people have the responsibility of making sure that once the book is printed and bound, it finds its way to the *wholesalers* (companies that buy books in bulk from publishers and sell directly to bookstores and other outlets), to such large bookstore chains as B. Dalton and Waldenbooks, and to the thousands of independent bookstores across the country.

Even when the book is on the shelves, an editor will continue to be the publishing house's main conduit of information about that book. Every time an author or agent inquires about royalties, a new printing, or the possibility of the book going out of print, the editor is the person who'll be contacted.

Beyond these responsibilities, he or she will also be expected to keep abreast of the field—visiting bookstores, researching new proposals to make sure they're legitimate and won't duplicate books already in print, and reading *Publisher's Weekly* to see what the competition is publishing. The editor must follow the activities of such organizations as the American Booksellers Association, the American Library Association, and the Association of American Publishers; and he or she must pay attention to lawsuits that involve publishers and details of First Amendment or copyright violations. The editor will inevitably be expected to peruse a sizable stack of trade journals, too.

Getting Started in Publishing

One editor (who prefers to remain anonymous) shared her view of editing with us. Her story typifies both the pains and pleasures of the publishing world:

"I was an editor of my high school and college newspapers, but then I tried to break into publishing and all they wanted was typing. Even my graduate degree meant little.

"I pounded the pavements for a while and then got my first job through an employment agency. I became an assistant to several editors. But there was no movement. At most houses, there's little movement.

"So I quit and went back to the employment agency. And, after a while, I became an assistant editor at Simon and Schuster. There, they promote every six months. But that is largely because, at a chaotic house, people leave regularly. There's an expression in publishing that you choose to work either at a frenetic pace to be promoted or for a sedate, prestigious publisher where you may never get promoted. At S and S, I started at $155 a week (in the mid-1970s). Eventually, I became a senior editor at a paperback house. And, of course, there was glamour: free lunches, free movies, free plays (after all, we occasionally did business with producers and playwrights). And there's the thrill of watching your book make the best-seller list.

"Also, there are parties: Authors throw themselves parties, publishers throw parties. The other day I attended an author's party given by a wealthy grandmother of the author. The house was huge, and there were Renoirs and Picassos on the walls."

I asked her what else was glamorous about being an editor, and she replied: "In all fairness, it *is* exciting to do books with celebrities—Michael Jackson, Candice Bergen, and others. And although many authors cause aggravation, many others are enjoyable to work with. If you think that being an editor at a publishing company means that you'll be working with James

Joyce, forget it! But it is rewarding to make a flawed manuscript into a well-polished book."

Occasionally, editors get fired or leave their jobs to become agents, publicists, or *packagers* (people who produce books by contracting directly with authors, designers, and illustrators before offering the book to a publisher as a complete "package"). The pressure of editorial responsibilities is not for everyone. Some disreputable publishers hire only young people because they can get away with paying them practically nothing and then keep only those who show unswerving devotion and who are willing to "marry" the job. One young editor, in a *Publisher's Weekly* roundup of job opportunities in the field, commented: "I'm committed to publishing, but I'm not sure that will continue when I'm thirty-five. What if I wanted to have a family? There would be no way it would be possible on this salary. It's a luxury to work in publishing as it is now, and I want to be paid for my ability."

In a *Publisher's Weekly* story announcing the retirement of Joan Manley—group vice president for books at Time-Life Books Inc. and a thirty-year publishing veteran—Manley was asked if she had any advice for women in publishing. "Women have always been in publishing and many have had distinguished careers," she said. "It offers more chance for equal opportunity and has a more substantial track record in that respect than, say, steel. The people who should stay in publishing are those who love it, despite gender. I guess my only advice is to enjoy it to the hilt, and, if you don't, get out. There's not that much money in it."

Achieving Success

As an editor, you need to set goals for yourself or you may be thought of as someone whom time has passed by. The best editors soon develop a maturity that makes them even tempered, reliable, and meticulous. They build solid relationships with agents and authors; they participate vigorously at editorial meetings; they take an interest in their colleagues and their colleagues' projects.

You'll work your way up by acquiring books that establish your reputation. They need not all sell fabulously well, but they should be books of quality, not just spinoffs of past ideas. Try to be well-rounded in your selections, since you don't want to get pigeonholed as the editor who does the humor books or the how-to books. You should be known as the person who has the imagination to develop any idea well—although it's also useful to develop several particular areas of expertise.

As you work your way up the ladder, you'll learn the value of "doing your homework" (i.e., researching potential book projects so that you can tell if an author's assessment of the book's competition is accurate). You'll learn how to cut through red tape at your publishing house, how to pitch your books at editorial meetings, and how to negotiate in such a way as to keep faith with agents and editors.

Not every editor wishes to progress to the high-paying, but administrative, job of editor-in-chief, but if you do wish to get there, don't be afraid to let your superiors know that you're on a fast track. They'll respect you for it.

In editing, success will lead to more success. As an editor's reputation grows, he or she will draw the attention of agents and authors. Soon, that editor will be offered more and better manuscripts. For some editors, the acquisition of a "hot" manuscript from a top author is a security blanket, a failure-proof trophy of success. Book buyers have a long memory, and when you hook up with best-selling authors, you have, in a sense, found a type of annuity: Your prestige grows with each new book the author writes.

Working for Smaller Publishers

The glamour of book publishing is not necessarily tied, however, to working at one of the larger, more prestigious houses. The advantage of these publishers is that they tend to have worked out efficient systems for conducting business. They take a professional attitude toward employee benefits, training, and mobility. But they do not guarantee that you'll be promoted or even noticed. And a small publisher may give you a better opportunity to see how the whole publishing process works. At St. Martin's Press, for example, it would not be unusual for an editor to wander into a publicist's office and chat informally about promotional plans for a new book.

If you're eager to get firsthand knowledge of how books are marketed, publicized, and sold, as well as edited, you may want to take a job with a publisher that has a relatively small staff, allowing entry-level assistants to share in the higher responsibilities and thus become more well rounded. Don't forget the world of independent small-press publishing. While most of the major houses are located in New York City, small presses are scattered throughout the country, and many of them provide well-rounded, responsible entry-level positions.

I've tried to be realistic in this brief look at publishing. There are a number of drawbacks that are hard to accept. Publishers know the allure of publishing, and the starting salaries seem to be more like honorariums. And the publishing world, relatively speaking, is small; sometimes the industry seems petty and unfair—rewarding tasteless trash with high advances and worthy books with an uncaring shrug. In its swing toward mass-marketing, mergers, and high advances, publishing may have lost some of its earlier charm, but it has also opened up a wide range of employment opportunities and widened the circle of people for whom reading is a lifetime joy. As an editor, even though you're behind the scenes, you can relish the satisfaction of walking through a bookstore and watching people discover and enjoy what you and an author worked so hard to achieve. Every book that touches the life of another person adds another drop of immortality to the author who wrote it—and to the editor who helped shape it.

Book Publishing: Required Reading

Every Sunday, the New York Times Book Review discusses about fifty of the most important new works in fiction, nonfiction, children's books, and poetry, as well as carrying features on major writers. A good review in the Times can pave the way to bestsellerdom. The Book Review is sold separately at many bookstores around the country and is available by subscription independent of the Sunday Times in which it appears. For subscriptions, write to the New York Times, Box 5792, GPO, New York, NY 10087.

Book World is the literary supplement to the Washington Post and has a circulation of one million. Although it reviews almost two thousand of the most significant new titles each year, it gives special attention to biographies and books on politics. In addition, it features columns on science fiction and on paperbacks. For subscriptions, write to the Washington Post, Washington, DC 20071.

Publisher's Weekly, the major trade magazine of the publishing industry, usually gives important new books their first review about six weeks in advance of the books' publication date (most other publications review books after publication). Each capsule review not only gives an overview of the book's plot but also summarizes any special distinction it may have, such as being a Book of the Month Club selection or having sold rights to a major magazine or film company.

The publishing world—and diligent book buyers—look forward to two special issues each year, the spring and fall announcements, which give a glimpse of books to come. In these two thick issues, major publishers advertise their book list for the new season. Leafing through these issues, an observant book fancier can learn exactly what the big books of the coming season will be and make book-buying plans accordingly. For subscriptions, write to R. R. Bowker & Co., 1180 Sixth Avenue, New York, NY 10036.

Examining more literary and scholarly books than other book-related publications, the *New York Review of Books* prides itself on provocative essays and interviews that address a variety of literary concerns. The twenty-year-old biweekly aims less at being timely than it does at being trenchant, and it has a flair for making odd-couple matchings of books and critics—Joan Didion on Woody Allen, for example. Gore Vidal, Susan Sontag, Tom Wicker, and Renata Adler are among its regular reviewers. For subscriptions, write to *The New York Review of Books*, 250 West Fifty-seventh Street, New York, NY 10019.

Two influential magazines of narrower scope are *Kirkus Reviews* and *Library Journal*. Founded in 1933, *Kirkus Reviews* is a thick compendium of reviews with no advertisements aimed at librarians. Published twenty-four times a year, each issue covers about two hundred titles, running the gamut of fiction and nonfiction, with occasional reviews of how-to books and children's titles. For subscriptions, write to *Kirkus Reviews*, 200 Park Avenue South, New York, NY 10003.

Library Journal, published twenty times a year, covers a wide range of fiction, non-fiction, technical, medical, and business titles. For subscriptions, write to *Library Journal*, 205 East Forty-second Street, New York, NY 10017.

Finally, two other top book-review supplements—the *Los Angeles Times Book Review* and the *Chicago Tribune Book Review*—are worth the price of a subscription to their parent publications. The *L.A. Times Book Review* has gained a national reputation in recent years, despite its occasional emphasis on California titles. For subscriptions, write to the *Los Angeles Times*, Times Mirror Square, Los Angeles, CA 90053.

The *Chicago Tribune's* Sunday book section reviews an unusually large number of paperbacks, both trade and mass-market. The reviews are national in scope and lively in tone. For subscriptions, write to the *Chicago Tribune*, Tribune Tower, Chicago, IL 60611.

A final note: Although not for the casual consumer, B. Dalton's "Hooked on Books" merchandise bulletin is perhaps the most powerful tastemaker in book retailing today. Written by Kay Sexton, Dalton's vice-president of marketing, "Hooked on Books" is supplied weekly to the managers of 704 B. Dalton stores around the country who, along with editors and salespeople in every major publishing house, read it to find out the latest publishing trends. B. Dalton's headquarters is One Corporate Center, 7505 Metro Boulevard, Minneapolis, MN 55435.

Fifty Prominent Book Publishers

The following publishers are among the most prominent in the field. Some have been chosen for their quality; others for the quantity of books they publish; others for the wide scope of their lists. Many of the publishers on this list seem to garner a disproportionate amount of media and trade-press attention for their books. If book publishing holds any glamour at all—and it does—you'll find a lot of that glamour attached to these houses:

Harry N. Abrams, Inc.
100 Fifth Ave.
New York, NY 10011

Ballantine Publishing Group
201 E. 50th St.
New York, NY 10022

Addison-Wesley
One Jacob Way
Reading, MA 01867

Bantam Books
1540 Broadway
New York, NY 10036

Arbor House Publishing Co.
235 E. 45th St.
New York, NY 10017

Atheneum Publishers
597 Fifth Ave.
New York, NY 10017

Avon Books
1350 Avenue of the Americas
New York, NY 10019

Dell Publishing
1540 Broadway
New York, NY 10036

Dodd Mead & Co
79 Madison Ave.
New York, NY 10016

Doubleday Books
1540 Broadway
New York, NY 10035

E.P. Dutton
2 Park Ave.
New York, NY 10016

M. Evans & Co., Inc.
216 E. 49th St.
New York, NY 10017

Facts on File
460 Park Ave. S.
New York, NY 10016

Berkley Publishing Group
200 Madison Ave.
New York, NY 10016

Crown Publishing Group
201 E. 50th St.
New York, NY 10022

Delacorte Press
One Dag Hammarskjold Plaza
New York, NY 10017

Harcourt Brace
525 B St., Suite 1900
San Diego, CA 92101

HarperCollins
10 E. 53rd St.
New York, NY 10022

Henry Holt and Company
115 W. 18th St.
New York, NY 10011

Houghton Mifflin Co.
215 Park Ave. S.
New York, NY 10003

Alfred A. Knopf/Random House
201 E. 50th St.
New York, NY 10022

The Linden Press
1230 Sixth Ave.
New York, NY 10020

Farrar, Straus & Giroux
19 Union Square West
New York, NY 10003

J. B. Lippincott
East Washington Square
Philadelphia, PA 19705

Franklin Watts
95 Madison Ave.
New York, NY 10016

Little, Brown & Co.
1271 Avenue of the Americas
New York, NY 10020

Grolier
95 Madison Ave.
New York, NY 10016

Macmillan General Reference
15 Columbus Circle
New York, NY 10023

Grove/Atlantic
841 Broadway
New York, NY 10003

McGraw-Hill
11 W. 19th St.
New York, NY 10011

William Morrow & Co.
1350 Avenue of the Americas
New York, NY 10016

Simon and Schuster
1230 Avenue of the Americas
New York, NY 10020

New American Library
1633 Broadway
New York, NY 10019

St. Martin's Press
175 Fifth Ave.
New York, NY 10012

W.W. Norton
500 Fifth Ave.
New York, NY 10110

Stein & Day
Scarborough House
Briarcliff Manor, NY 10510

Oxford University Press
200 Madison Ave.
New York, NY 10016

Ten Speed Press
Box 7123
Berkeley, CA 94707

Pocket Books
1230 Avenue of the Americas
New York, NY 10020

Ticknor & Fields
383 Orange St.
New Haven, CT 06511

Price/Stern/Sloan
410 N. La Cienega Blvd.
Los Angeles, CA 90048

Putnam Publishing Group
200 Madison Ave.
New York, NY 10016

Random House, Inc.
201 E. 50th St.
New York, NY 10022

Reader's Digest Books
Reader's Digest Rd.
Pleasantville, NY 10750

Scholastic, Inc.
555 Broadway
New York, NY 10012

Time-Life Books, Inc
777 Duke St.
Alexandria, VA 22314

Viking Press
40 W. 23rd St.
New York, NY 10010

Warner Books
1271 Avenue of the Americas
New York, NY 10020

John Wiley & Sons
605 Third Ave.
New York, NY 10158

Workman Publishing
708 Broadway
New York, NY 10003

Selected Employment Agencies That Specialize in Book Publishing

Abie Personnel
280 Madison Ave.
New York, NY 10016

Helen Akullian Agency
280 Madison Ave.
New York, NY 10016

Hadle Agency
535 Fifth Ave.
York, NY 10017

Lynne Palmer
739 Boylston St., Suite 400
Boston, MA 02117

Career Blazers
500 Fifth Ave.
New York, NY 10036

Lynne Palmer
14 E. 60th St.
New York, NY 10022

Bert Davis Associates
400 Madison Ave.
New York, NY 10017

Lyman Personnel Service
3820 Buffalo Speedway
Suite 110
Houston, TX 77028

Mary Diehl Placement Bureau
50 E. 42nd St., #308
New York, NY 10017

Remer-Ribolow Agency, Inc.
507 Fifth Ave.
New York, NY 10036

Editorial Experts Inc.
Employment Service
444 N. Michigan, Suite 870
Chicago, IL 60611

Roth Young of Chicago
5905 Pratt St.
Alexandria, VA 22310

Gardner Personnel, Inc.
300 Madison Ave.
New York, NY 10016

Publishing: A Brief Glossary

Advance. An amount of money advanced to the author by the publisher before publication of the book. The advance is subtracted from royalties earned from the book's future sales.

Author tour. A promotion trip, usually arranged by the publisher, to help an author generate interest in his or her book throughout the country.

Back-list. A book, often with a limited audience, published with the expectation of selling a steady number of copies over a period of years.

Breakout potential. A book with breakout potential is expected to "break out" of a particular subject or genre category to attract readers from other areas of interest, or to attract a significant number of new readers and sell much better than the author's earlier books.

First printing. The number of copies printed when a book is first published.

Front-list. All the new books presented in a selling season.

Galleys. Bound or unbound, these typeset proofs are shown to authors to help correct errors in format and content. *Bound galleys* are also sent to magazines, newspapers, and other reviewers for evaluation in advance of or concurrent with publication.

Hopes 'n' Dreams book. A term for a book that appeals to the hopes and dreams of readers rather than to realistic practicalities.

Impulse buy. A book placed close to the cash register at a store so that buyers may purchase it on impulse. Often displayed in a publisher-supplied countertop unit called a *prepack*.

LMP. Literary Market Place.

Mass-market paperback. A rack-size paperback book aimed at a mass audience, usually printed in quantities of twenty-five thousand or more.

Mid-list. A fiction or nonfiction book that is neither as specialized as a back-list book nor as conspicuous as a front-list book, with an identifiable audience and a well-known author.

Multiple submissions. Submitting a book manuscript to several publishers at once instead of one at a time.

Packager. A person who arranges the elements of a book—idea, manuscript, production—and packages all elements, either to submit them to a publisher or to produce the book independently.

PW. Publisher's Weekly, the trade magazine considered to be the bible of publishing.

Reprint rights. The rights that a publisher buys in order to be allowed to reprint a hardcover book in a paperback format (a.k.a. paperback rights).

Royalty. Money (usually representing a certain percentage of sales) paid to an author in compensation for the continuing right to publish and sell his or her book.

Run. The number of copies printed at any one time. A trade hardcover's first run might average five thousand to fifteen thousand copies, while a mass-market paperback's first printing might be twenty-five thousand to fifty thousand copies.

Serial rights. The right to serialize or run excerpts from a book, usually a new book. First serial rights give the right to excerpt part of a book *before* the book is officially published. Second serial rights give the right to excerpt a book *following* the book's publication. Only a small number of magazines buy first serial rights to books. These rights, often expensive, can generate excellent publicity for a new book while attracting new readers to the magazine running the excerpt.

Stocking stuffer. A low-priced, often whimsical book that publishers promote as a possible gift item. These books usually have wide appeal (e.g., *The Preppy Handbook, Items from Our Catalogue* and *Dieter's Guide to Weight Loss During Sex*).

Sub rights. Subsidiary rights, including reprint, serial, translation, book-club, performance, and other rights in a book, beyond its presentation in its original form.

Syndication rights. The right to syndicate a portion of a new book—to edit the excerpt and distribute it to a newspaper syndicate's network of affiliated newspapers.

Trade book. A book that is published for the general public and sold at bookstores (as distinct from textbooks, which are marketed to schools).

Magazine Writing

Magazines on the Rise

In today's information society, the media of communication are changing at a rapid pace. Where once magazine racks held a small selection of periodicals dominated by such giants as *Life* and *Look,* today there are magazines aimed at every special interest group, technical field, hobby, industry, and discipline imaginable. For example, there is a magazine just for hog farmers and another for people who treat sludge. There are magazines for IBM PC users, Macintosh users, Windows users, Lotus 1-2-3 users, UNIX users, and IBM AS/400 users.

Magazines combine news with how-to information and advice. They are designed to help you do whatever you like to do better, whether it's run, bicycle, play volleyball, program computers, macrame, lift weights, eat gourmet foods, or garden. Because they target specific interests, a larger percentage of their content is of interest to their readers than is the content of a daily newspaper.

Today there are more than fourteen thousand magazines published in the United States. These include not only general-interest and consumer magazines, but also scholarly journals, trade publications, and special-interest magazines.

With this many magazines, there is an enormous opportunity for both free-lance and staff writing positions. In fact, producing magazine articles serves as a source of income for more writers than any other type of writing. When you read writers' magazines such as *Writer's Digest* and the *Writer,* you will find more articles on writing for magazines than any other topic.

Magazines: Where to Find Them

An amazing number of people want to write for magazines they have never seen, much less read. This is a mistake. A magazine is like a potential employer and can easily be studied. Just buy some copies at a newsstand or check a few out of the local library.

Many magazines sell sample issues and offer free writer's guidelines. Send for both. Study the publication. The only reason to work for a magazine covering a subject that doesn't excite you is to get experience, so eventually you can get the job you really want.

Your library has several reference books that list magazines, including *Reader's Guide to Periodical Literature*, *Writer's Market*, *Bacon's Publicity Checker*, and *Standard Rate and Data Service*. Of these, *Writer's Market* is most oriented toward writers and provides such useful information as addresses, the names of managing editors, what percentage of the editorial content is produced by staff versus free-lance written, and the types of articles the magazines publish.

Writer's Market categorizes magazines as either consumer or trade. Consumer magazines, such as *Family Circle*, *Reader's Digest*, and *Glamour*, are read by the general public. Trade magazines, which include business and technical journals, are read by specialists in business or technical fields. Most writers want to work for consumer magazines, and consumer magazines generally pay better. On the other hand, there are many more trade magazines, so competition is less fierce.

Magazine Staff Writer

The best way to learn the positions available at magazines is to look at their mastheads. Some magazines have editors on staff and use free-lancers to do the writing. Other magazines have multiple editors and staff writers who produce a large portion of the magazine's "editorial" (industry jargon for articles as opposed to ads, which are written by advertisers and their ad agencies).

Most magazines use some combination of staff and free-lance talent. A staff writer at a major consumer magazine can earn $40,000 a year or more. At trade publications, salaries range from $20,000 a year to $40,000 a year or more. Some trade journals pay dismally while others will surprise you, offering salaries near to or in excess of many consumer magazines.

Consumer magazines generally want to hire editors and writers with some journalism experience, typically with newspapers or another magazine. A consumer electronics publication, for example, would more likely be interested in an applicant who wrote on the same subject for an electronics trade journal. Trade experience is valuable and a good stepping-stone to consumer publications. Sometimes magazines will hire people who have been publicists or free-lancers.

You may not start as a writer. Magazines often hire editorial assistants at salaries in the mid- to high-teens, and this is one way to break in. The *New Yorker* is famous for hiring aspiring writers as fact-checkers and having them later become famous authors. Some magazines, like *Mademoiselle*, have intern programs that hire college journalism majors for summer jobs. Often an internship can result in a job offer after school.

Trade journals hire editors and staff writers of two types. The first is the English-major type, who is primarily a writer and has no particular expertise in the industry or field covered by the publication. These writers are hired for their writing skills and often spend time turning manuscripts submitted by business executives, engineers, and scientists into readable articles.

The second type of writer hired by trade publications is the technical expert who has worked in the industry and wants to change careers to get into writing and journalism. These people are hired more for their contacts and industry knowledge, although writing talent, even if raw, is still desired.

If you are an expert in a subject matter, such as the Internet or chemical engineering, it may be easier for you to get a staff position with a trade journal than for a writer who is a generalist and has no such experience. For example, after college, I was unable to get an interview with any newspaper because I hadn't studied journalism or done any newspaper writing (aside from my college newspaper). But *Chemical Engineering Progress,* a trade journal, gave me an interview, even though I had no magazine experience, because my degree was in chemical engineering.

Free-Lance Writer

Of the thousands of magazines published today, a large majority buy articles from free-lance writers. The key to getting free-lance assignments to write for magazines is not a cover letter or resume. It is a query letter. If you can master writing query letters, you can get article assignments from magazines.

A query letter is, in essence, a sales letter. The prospect is the editor. The product you want to sell the editor is not you—it is the article you want to write for the magazine.

Editors look for professionalism in query letters. This means no typos, no misspellings. Address the letter to a specific editor by name, and spell his or her name right.

Another thing editors look for is familiarity with the magazine. Don't suggest an article on hunting elk to the newsletter for the ASPCA. Sounds obvious, but such things happen every day; for example, writers often make the mistake of proposing "how-to" articles to magazines that don't do "how-to." Study the market before you send your query.

Editors also look for good writing. If you can, write the first paragraph or two of your query so it could be used, as is, as the lead for your article. This shows the editor that you know how to begin a piece and get the reader's attention.

In addition, editors dislike lazy writers—those who want to see their by-lines in a magazine but refuse to do research or get their facts straight. Put a lot of hard "nuts-and-bolts" information—facts, figures, statistics—in your letter to show the editor that you know your subject. Most query letters (and articles) are too light on content.

Credentials impress editors. Tell the editor why he or she should hire you to write the article. If you are an expert in the subject, say so. If not, describe your sources. Tell which experts you will interview, which studies you will cite, which references you will consult. Also, list your previous publishing credentials, if you have any—especially books and articles in well-known magazines.

Estimate the length of your article in terms of the number of words. The *Writer's Market* listings usually include a magazine's preferred word count. Articles range in length from two hundred-word fillers to five thousand-word features. The average length of magazine articles today seems to be in the range of fifteen hundred to two thousand words, or about six to eight double-spaced typed pages.

The more fully developed your idea, the better. If you spell out everything—your topic, your approach, an outline, your sources, the expected length of the article—then editors know what they will get when they give you the go-ahead to write the piece. The more complete your query, the better your chance for a sale.

The following are sample query letters. All were successful and resulted in an assignment to write an article. All articles were accepted and have been published.

Mr. Kenneth J. McNaughton
Associate Editor
Chemical Engineering
McGraw-Hill Building
1221 Avenue of the Americas
New York, NY 10020

Dear Mr. McNaughton:

When a chemical engineer can't write a coherent report, the true value of his investigation or study may be distorted or unrecognized. His productivity vanishes. And his chances for career advancement diminish.

As an associate editor of *Chemical Engineering*, you know that many chemical engineers could use some help in improving their technical writing skills. I'd like to provide that help by writing an article that gives your readers "Ten Tips for Better Business Writing."

An outline of the article is attached. This two-thousand-word piece would provide ten helpful tips—each less than two hundred words—to help chemical engineers write better letters, reports, proposals, and articles.

Tip number three, for example, instructs writers to be more concise. Too many engineers would write about an "accumulation of particulate matter about the peripheral interior surface of the vessel" when they're describing solids buildup. And how many managers would use the phrase "until such time as" when they simply mean "until"?

My book, *Technical Writing: Structure, Standards, and Style*, will be published by the McGraw-Hill Book Company in November. While the book speaks to a wide range of technical disciplines, my article will draw its examples from the chemical engineering literature.

I hold a B.S. in chemical engineering from the University of Rochester and am a member of the American Institute of Chemical Engineers. Until this past January, I was manager of marketing communications for Koch Engineering, a manufacturer of chemical process equipment. Now, I'm an independent copywriter specializing in industrial advertising.

Ken, I'd like to write "Ten Tips for Better Technical Writing" for your "You and Your Job" section. How does this sound?

Sincerely,

Bob Bly

Article Outline
TEN TIPS FOR BETTER TECHNICAL WRITING
by Robert W. Bly

1. Know your readers. Are you writing for engineers? Managers? Laymen?
2. Write in a clear, conversational style. Write to express—not to impress.
3. Be concise. Avoid wordiness. Omit words that do not add to your meaning.
4. Be consistent ... especially in the use of numbers, symbols, and abbreviations.
5. Use jargon sparingly. Use technical terms only when there are no simpler words that can better communicate your thoughts.
6. Avoid big words. Do not write "utilize" when "use" will do just as well.
7. Prefer the specific to the general. Technical readers are interested in solid technical information and not in generalities. Be specific.
8. Break the writing up into short sections. Short sections, paragraphs, and sentences are easier to read than long ones.
9. Use visuals. Graphs, tables, photos, and drawings can help get your message across.

10. Use the active voice. Write "John performed the experiment," not "The experiment was performed by John." The active voice adds vigor to writing.

The letter and brief outline give the editor plenty of information on which to base a decision. The letter clearly states the need for the article, as well as the writer's credentials, both as a writer and in the field of technical writing.

Mr. William Brohaugh
Editor
Writers Digest
9933 Alliance Road
Cincinnati, Ohio 45242

Dear Mr. Brohaugh:

John Frances Tighe, a soft-spoken, bearded gentleman, modestly refers to himself as "the world's second-most successful free-lance direct-mail copywriter."

John's fee for writing a direct-mail package? $15,000.

But that's peanuts compared to the $40,000 Henry Cowan charges. According to *Who's Mailing What*, a newsletter covering the direct-mail industry, Cowan is the highest paid copywriter in the world. *Direct Marketing* magazine reports that his income on the Publisher's Clearing House mailing alone (for which he receives a royalty) was $900,000 in a recent year.

Next to the movies and best-selling novels, direct mail is one of the highest-paid markets for free-lance writers. Although surprisingly easy to break into, it's an industry most free-lancers don't even know about. Direct-mail writing is dominated by a few dozen writers who earn lush six-figure incomes writing only a few days a week.

I'd like to write a three-thousand-word article on "Making Money as a Direct-Mail Writer." The article would tell your readers everything they need to know to start getting assignments in this lucrative but little-known specialty.

Here are the topics I would cover:

1. THE SECRET WORLD OF DIRECT MAIL. What is direct mail? Who is writing direct mail—and how much are they earning? Why has this market been a secret until now? I would interview some old pros as well as some new writers to get their perspectives.

2. A LOOK AT THE MARKET. What are the various uses of direct mail (mail order, fund-raising, lead generation, cordial contact)? Types and formats of direct-mail packages you might write. Types of organizations that hire free-lance writers (publishers, catalog houses, fund-raisers, insurance companies, banks, manufacturers, ad agencies) and how (and where) to find them.

3. GETTING STARTED. Learning about direct mail. Studying the market. Building your swipe files. Getting your first assignments.

4. HOW TO WRITE DIRECT-MAIL COPY THAT SELLS. Understanding the mission of direct mail. Tips for writing copy that will get results. How to present your copy to clients. Graphics and layouts for direct-mail copy. Differences in sales copy (direct mail) versus editorial copy (magazine writing).

5. MARKETING YOUR SERVICES. Getting and keeping clients. How to market your services using: Portfolios. Meetings. Telephone calls. Letters. Advertising. Publicity techniques.

6. FEES. How to set fees. Table of typical fees. What others charge.

7. KEEPING UP WITH THE FIELD. Books. Publications. Professional organizations. Courses. Seminars.

This article will draw both from my own experience as a successful direct-mail copywriter (clients include Prentice-Hall, New York Telephone, Hearst, Chase Manhattan, Edith Roman Associates) and from interviews with top pros in the field—including Milt Pierce, Sig Rosenblum, Richard Armstrong, Don Hauptman, Andrew Linick, and others. I know these people personally, so getting the interviews is no problem.

Also, I am a member of the Direct Marketing Club of New York and author of the forthcoming book, *Direct Mail Profits* (Asher-Gallant Press).

May I proceed with the article as outlined?

An SASE is enclosed. Thanks for your consideration.

Regards,

Bob Bly

SASE in the last sentence stands for "self-addressed stamped envelope." Including an SASE is a must for every query letter and manuscript submission.

Mr. James A. Frank, Editor
AMTRAK EXPRESS
34 East 51st Street
New York, NY 10022

Dear Mr. Frank:

Is this letter a waste of paper?

Yes—if it fails to get the desired result.

In business, most letters and memos are written to generate a specific response—close a sale, set up a meeting, get a job interview, make a contact. Many of these letters fail to do their job.

Part of the problem is that business executives and support staff don't know how to write persuasively. The solution is a formula first discovered by advertising copywriters—a formula called AIDA. AIDA stands for Attention, Interest, Desire, Action.

First, the letter gets Attention...with a hard-hitting lead paragraph that goes straight to the point or offers an element of intrigue.

Then, the letter hooks the reader's Interest. The hook is often a clear statement of the reader's problem, needs, or desires. If you are writing to a customer who received damaged goods, state the problem. And then promise a solution.

Next, create Desire. You are offering something—a service, a product, an agreement, a contract, a compromise, a consultation. Tell the reader the benefit he'll receive from your offering. Create a demand for your product.

Finally, call for Action. Ask for the order, the signature, the check, the assignment.

I'd like to give you a fifteen-hundred-word article on "How to Write Letters That Get Results." The piece will illustrate the AIDA formula with a variety of actual letters and memos from insurance companies, banks, manufacturers, and other organizations.

This letter, too, was written to get a specific result—an article assignment from the editor of *Amtrak Express*.

Did it succeed?

Regards,

Bob Bly

P.S. By way of introduction, I'm an advertising consultant and the author of five books, including *Technical Writing: Structure, Standards, and Style* (McGraw-Hill).

Whether you want a staff position or prefer the variety and independence of free-lancing, you'll need to develop a portfolio and resume that demonstrate your ability to write, generate ideas, and target your ideas to a specific audience.

If you have expertise or interest in a specific topic, you can make yourself indispensible to an editor by presenting a number of article ideas you'd like to pursue. When you're just starting to build your portfolio, the response to your queries might ask that you write the article you suggest "on spec." That guarantees that at least the article will be read, that the editor is interested in the idea. But it doesn't necessarily mean that the article will be purchased and published. The editor wants to be sure you can deliver an article that will fit well with the magazine's content, writing style, and tone. Even magazines that don't pay, or pay only in contributors' copies or a small honorarium, require that you send a query letter before they will assign an article to you.

Magazine editors are always looking for new ideas. Filling the pages of a magazine every month requires the efforts and talents of many individuals. If you're an "idea person," someone who can come up with viable ideas and match them to the appropriate publications, you'll be off to a good start in a magazine career.

Stringers

Being a stringer is not a career. Rather, it's a way for writers and others interest in the printed word to earn extra money by being involved in the magazine field. Newspapers also use stringers; in fact, they use them more than magazines do.

A stringer is someone who looks for hot tips, leads, and story ideas and brings them to the attention of the appropriate editors. The stringer may just supply the idea or more detailed background information on the story or even be asked to do some legwork or research.

If the idea develops into an article, the stringer is paid a fee. This is usually a nominal sum, but not always. Some of the tabloids, most notably the *National Enquirer*, pay a fairly decent fee for story leads.

Story ideas submitted by stringers are turned over to staff or free-lance writers, although if you've developed a good relationship with the magazine as a free-lancer you will often be given the assignment. Being a stringer can provide the opportunity to get free-lance assignments or even a staff position.

Stringers do not generally get by-lines for having provided an article idea. Therefore, if an idea or tip you gave a magazine becomes an article, you cannot claim to have been published in that magazine unless you wrote the article yourself.

The CompuServe Journalism Forum has a message board concerned solely with stringers and free-lancing. For more information, call CompuServe toll-free 800-858-0411.

Education and Experience

There is no specific educational requirement for magazine writing. Unlike newspapers, which greatly favor applicants with journalism degrees, magazines don't particularly favor journalism majors. So the lack of a degree in this field is not a handicap here.

The best way to sell yourself as a magazine writer, aside from query letters, is clippings of articles you have written. The more articles you get published, the more clippings or tear sheets you have to send editors. This is why many writers, at the beginning of their careers, will write for smaller and specialized publications at no charge, simply to get the by-line and clippings. This is something you'll stop once you begin to get paid for your writing, but there is nothing wrong with doing it when you start.

Resources

Periodicals

AWP Chronicle. Associated Writing Programs, Old Dominion University, Norfolk, VA 23529.

Freelance Writer's Report. Cassell Communications, P.O. Box 9844, Fort Lauderdale, FL 33310.

Writer's Digest. F&W Publications, 1507 Dana Ave., Cincinnati, OH 45207.

Books and Directories

Elane Feldman. *The Writer's Guide to Self-Promotion and Publicity.*Cincinnati, OH: Writer's Digest Books. 1990.

Literary Market Place. R.R. Bowker Company, 249 W. 17th St., New York, NY 10011. Annual.*The Writer's Market*. Cincinnati, OH: Writer's Digest Books. Annual.

Pattis, S. William. *Opportunities in Magazine Publishing Careers*. Lincolnwood, IL: VGM Career Horizons, 1992.

Todd, Alden . *Finding Facts Fast: How to Find Out What You Want and Need to Know*. Berkeley, CA: Ten Speed Press, 1983.

CHAPTER   FOUR

Writing for Newspapers

*I*t is difficult—not impossible, but difficult—to get a job in journalism without having majored in the subject at college. Therefore, if you are interested in becoming a reporter, this should be your major course of study at school.

The other requirement is that you were active in your high school and college newspapers. This is how you generate published writing samples—known in the business as "clips" or "clippings"—to show editors who can hire you for your first newspaper job.

The reason it's hard to get a job without these credentials is that the field is so competitive. So many young people want to be reporters and editors, there are many more applicants than there are jobs. Those who have the education and the experience have the advantage.

There are exceptions. Expertise in a specific field may substitute for experience in journalism, if the specialty is in demand. For instance, one writer was asked to be a financial reporter, even though his previous job experience was in real estate because he had written a book on the subject. The book demonstrated both his expertise in the subject and his writing ability, but his experience is the exception, not the rule.

Another way to get both clips and experience is to write for your town's local weekly newspaper or shopper. These newspapers pay little or nothing for unsolicited articles, but they are real newspapers, and the experience and the published news clipping will help begin to establish your credentials as a journalist. Many big-city newspaper reporters and editors began their careers on the staffs of weekly newspapers. While many move on to careers on larger newspapers, others stay to advance in editorial positions. They like the small-town flavor and the focus on local news and issues.

My Own Story

I didn't plan for a career in journalism; I wasn't even on my high school newspaper. But in college, I became addicted to newspaper writing while on the staff of the school's daily newspaper. In my senior year, despite having majored in chemical engineering, not journalism, and having taken only one English course (Dickens), I decided to try to get a newspaper job.

I wrote to one hundred newspapers and received not one positive reply. The fact that I did not have a journalism degree was a major drawback. The former editor of our college paper, a friend, had become a reporter. He arranged for me to interview with the Associated Press in Buffalo, New York. I failed the spelling test and did not get a job offer.

A couple of articles written for my school paper were picked up and run in a local newspaper in Rochester, New York. I took a staff job as a corporate writer with Westinghouse in Baltimore, but still yearned to write for newspapers.

Baltimore had an "alternative" paper called the *City Paper*— its equivalent of Manhattan's *Village Voice*. I called the editor, told him I wanted to write feature articles, and arranged for an appointment.

He assigned several articles to me over the course of the next year, ranging from book reviews to feature stories on drag racing and radio evangelism. I did my best to imitate Hunter S. Thompson and wrote them in a New Journalism style. I was very excited to be doing this type of writing and getting it published—it was in sharp contrast to my more conservative corporate work writing brochures on radars and electronic communications systems. The pay was meager, $25 per article, but I enjoyed the writing.

My personal career took a different turn as I became more involved in corporate writing and advertising copywriting. While these are more lucrative career options than newspaper journalism, for many the excitement and responsibility of being part of the Fourth Estate is worth the trade-off.

The Fourth Estate

In the United States, the First Amendment to the Constitution established a unique role for American journalism—to be an unofficial watchdog of the government. An informed citizenry is at the heart of a democracy, and a free press was seen as essential to providing the people with access to information about their elected officials. In essence, the press became a branch of the American system of government—known in press circles as "The Fourth Estate"—reporting to the populace the activities of the senate, the judiciary, and the presidency.

The best journalists take the responsibility that comes with the right to a free press very much to heart. That responsibility requires reporting accurate, reliable news with the purpose of informing the populace.

Working for Newspapers

The newspaper business is deadline driven. As a newspaper reporter, you learn to write and edit quickly. Daily newspapers need fresh stories every day. So newspaper writers work on incredibly tight deadlines.

Reporters for small newspapers cover everything from local town council meetings to high school sports, obituaries to crime reports. The size of the staff usually means you're an all-purpose reporter. This is a great opportunity to learn the trade and can be more interesting to someone who prefers a variety of subjects about which to write.

On larger newspapers, reporters generally specialize on a "beat." Like the cop who walks a beat and gets to know the neighborhood, a beat reporter gets to know all the necessary background and contacts for covering a specific subject area. Some of the usual beats are police, courts, education, business, entertainment, or sports.

Although newspapers do publish feature stories, most of what is in newspapers has a news slant. You must be aware of what is going on within your beat, whether it's the PTA, the city council, the city police desk, or the world. If current events do not fascinate you, and you are not already an avid newspaper reader, you might be better off doing a type of writing that interests and fascinates you more.

The News Cycle

Whether you work for a large daily or a small weekly, the news cycle begins with getting your reporting assignments from an editor. On a smaller paper, usually only one or two people have "editor" as part of their title. If you're on a daily paper, you'll get your assignments from the editor of your section or beat, such as the city editor or the sports editor. If you happen upon a story on your own, you'll need to clear it with the editor.

It's the role of the editor to determine what is newsworthy. Often the editor will dictate an "angle" or "slant" to your story—how to approach it or what viewpoint to take. On larger papers, the editors of various sections meet daily with the managing editor to discuss what each section will carry in the next day's newspaper.

Once your articles are written, they are reviewed by the editor and, at large newspapers, by the copyeditors who check your writing for errors and proper newspaper style. Most newspapers follow the style set by the Associated Press and outlined in the *The Associated Press Stylebook and Libel Manual*.

The whole cycle—getting story ideas, assigning reporters to cover them, writing the articles and editing them—is repeated daily, or weekly. For some, the cycle can get monotonous, but for many others, the constant demand for news and the pace of meeting deadlines is exciting.

Learning to Write Newspaper Articles

You will have an enormous advantage in your search for a newspaper career if you already know how to write a newspaper article before you apply for a job.

Writing newspaper articles is like playing the piano: It's relatively simple to learn the basics and turn out an acceptable article, but you can then spend the rest of your life refining your craft.

There are two ways to learn about writing for newspapers. The first is in school, either by taking journalism courses or by working on your school paper, or both. High school journalism courses are valuable and can teach you a lot, but a bachelor's degree in journalism is a good idea if you want to pursue this as a career.

Another option, if you have a bachelor's degree in another field, is to go to graduate school in journalism. Many colleges and universities offer degree programs in journalism. One of the most highly respected program is that of the Columbia University Graduate School of Journalism, (709F Journalism Building,

New York, NY 10027). Another is the University of Missouri School of Journalism, the oldest such program in the country (Columbia, MO 65211).

The second way to learn about journalism is to write articles for practice. Perhaps you have a club or company newsletter. Ask the editor if you can contribute some articles. Small weekly community shoppers occasionally take articles from town residents. Many weekly and some daily papers also accept freelance article submissions. Pay is minimal, often $50 or less per article. One local columnist, when on vacation, is able to get temporary replacements to write her parenting column at no charge—seeing their by-lines in the newspaper is payment enough.

The best way to free-lance for newspapers is to send query letters, as with magazines. Look at the kinds of articles the newspaper publishes. Study the organization and writing style. Then come up with your own ideas that you think will fit in with the newspaper's format. You can present your ideas to the editor first in the form of a query letter or telephone call, or you can take a chance and write the article to submit "on spec"— on the spculation that the editor will like it enough to publish it. Chapter 2 presents detailed instructions on how to write query letters that get article assignments.

Developing a Specialty

One way to launch a journalism career without a lot of journalism experience is by specializing in a subject matter, such as science, technology, computers, business, real estate, investments, travel, or other topics.

Are you an expert? Do you give seminars, work in a particular field, or have advanced credentials in a field routinely covered by the press? Approach local newspapers to see if they need a science, medical, or consumer reporter covering your particular specialty. Some editors will hire journalists who have proven subject expertise or expert credentials, even if their journalism experience or writing background is limited.

Of course, you'll improve your chances by both becoming a subject expert and getting known as a writer who specializes in that field. If you have authored a gardening book, for example, you may be able to convince your town paper to have you do a weekly column on gardening and lawn care. That column can be syndicated to other newspapers, and the experience can help you get hired by larger papers that pay better salaries.

Chapter 2 discusses writing for trade journals and other specialized professional publications. Newspapers often hire trade journal editors and reporters to cover a particular beat or field related to the topic of their journal. This is a good career path, as it is much easier for a beginner to get a writing job with a trade journal than with a newspaper. One college friend, who majored in electrical engineering and started working for an electrical engineering magazine after college, is now a successful newspaper bureau chief in London.

Getting Started

The more experience you gain in high school, college, or freelance writing before you start applying for your first job, the more quickly you will be hired as a reporter. Geographic mobility is also a plus.

When you begin your job search, send cover letters and resumes to a broad range of newspapers, some to national papers, some to large city dailies, and others to town weeklies. There are more than six thousand newspapers in the United States. Send out two hundred to three hundred resumes in your first mailing wave. With phone follow ups, expect this to yield two to five interviews, and if you're fortunate, a job. If no job is offered, send another three hundred resumes and repeat the process. Tenacity pays off in getting jobs as well as news stories.

The cover letter should highlight journalism education and experience as well as any specialized subject knowledge. If you have published articles in magazines, say so. If you are a published book author, this will impress potential employers even more.

Newspaper writing is probably the most difficult specialty to break into. You may have to start small, writing for town weeklies. Do not turn up your nose at this. It is an excellent opportunity that opens the path to a career working for more prestigious publications. And the smaller and more local the newspaper, the less competitive it will be.

Start Small

Certainly small newspapers have different standards than the *Boston Globe* or the *New York Times*. While some aspiring journalists view the small-town weekly as the bottom of the barrel, I disagree. Newspaper writing seems simple, but experienced journalists know they are learning and improving with every piece they write. Writing for a small town paper can give you excellent experience and credentials that get you a job on a larger paper. Smaller papers offer a mix of journalism, blending local politics with articles that are almost promotional in the way they advertise library sales, parades, Litle League, club meetings, and other hometown events.

If you decide to work for a smaller paper, do it with enthusiasm. Yes, there will be "puff pieces" to write. But you will also have the opportunity to cover local government, events, news, and community affairs in an intelligent, even sophisticated, fashion. Do both types of articles as required, and do your best. That's the way to learn your craft and get clippings you can use to secure a better job down the road.

Networking

Becoming involved in the media world and the community of journalists can give you the contacts you need to open the door to a newspaper job. An excellent way to start is by joining the American Society of Journalists and Authors (1501 Broadway, Suite 302, New York, NY 10036). Attend meetings to meet and network with fellow writers as well as editors who can buy freelance material or hire you for a staff position. The society also has a job hotline for members that can bring you work. Call or write for information today.

Switching Fields

It's easier to get into many of the other writing specialties discussed in this book than to break into newspaper journalism.

Therefore, a good strategy is to start in another area of writing, establish credentials and clippings, then move from that field into journalism. Many journalists are former publicists, press agents, magazine writers, book authors, technical editors, or corporate writers. Conversely, many journalists often go into these other fields when they tire of the low pay that is typical at many newspapers.

Even if you have a nonwriting job, you can and should moonlight or free-lance if you want to switch careers and become a reporter. The more writing samples and clips you have, the better your chances of being hired.

If money becomes an issue and you can't get into a bigger paper, you may consider switching to a better-paying field, such as public relations or corporate communications. Some journalists consider these viable career options, while others feel they are selling out. It's up to you.

Another career path is to move from newspapers to broadcast—radio or television. Although smaller radio and cable TV stations pay surprisingly modest salaries, on-camera personalities for broadcast channels can make big money—$100,000 to

$350,000 a year or more! Some reporters continue to write for newspapers while doing TV or radio commentary in addition to their writing, giving them the best of both worlds.

Free-Lancing

Magazines offer much more opportunity for free-lancing than newspapers. Most newspaper writers are on staff, not free-lance. Yes, some newspapers hire free-lancers, but the work is sporadic and the pay is minimal. I do not know a single free-lance writer who makes a living writing exclusively or primarily for newspapers. For more on free-lancing for magazines, see Chapter 2.

Large daily newspapers that circulate over a broad geographic region often higher "stringers"—experienced reporters who work on a free-lance basis from a region covered by the newspaper. The reporter often sells the story to both the large daily paper and a smaller local newspaper. If the story has an even broader news value, it might be picked up by a wire service as well.

The Wire Services

Many reporters got their start in the news business by selling stories to one of the wire services. A wire service is a news agency that distributes news stories to papers all over the country, originally over telegraph wires but now through telephone wires via fax or modem.

The most widely recognized wire service is the Associated Press. Smaller but well-distributed agencies include the Cox News Service, the New York Times News Service, and Knight-Ridder News Service. You'll find these and other wire services in the directories listed at the end of this chapter.

From Reporter to Editor

Many reporters climb the career ladder by becoming editors. An editor assigns stories, manages a staff of reporters, edits copy, and is responsible for the content of the newspaper. There is more management responsibility and slightly more money. As an editor, you will do more editing and managing and less investigative reporting and writing.

You will not start in this business as an editor. Your first job will be as a reporter. Within the ranks of the reporters, you can assume more and more responsibility and autonomy. If you do well, eventually you may be offered an editor's position. Or you can apply when a position opens up on your paper or a competing paper.

Writing Columns

Most daily newspapers have staff columnists who write on subjects ranging from politics and foreign affairs to consumerism and investing. Often columnists write for one paper and have the column syndicated so that it runs in many other papers nationwide. Jane Applegate, for example, writes a column for the *LA Times* that appears several times a week in the business section of my local daily paper, the *Record*.

National syndication is a ticket to success in a big way for many writers. It is not exactly easy to achieve but is probably less difficult than most writers believe.

Most people are aware that such well-known columnists as Carl Rowan, James Kilpatrick, and William Buckley are nationally syndicated—they sell their columns regularly to newspapers all over the country. Not so well known, probably, is that it is not only political columnists and "big names" whose columns are syndicated in this manner. Writers of "service" columns are also widely syndicated—"Dear Abby" is the most familiar example, but there are also Sylvia Porter, Rona Barrett, Eliot Janeway, and many others—many not nearly so well known—writing on personal problems, household hints, finance and economics, investment, medical matters, career concerns, and other topics.

Even this is not a complete list of the types of materials that may be syndicated. The crossword puzzles, comic strips, political cartoons, and other such items in your newspaper are also syndicated.

In short, almost anything that would interest newspaper readers generally may be syndicated, including completely new ideas.

The market is both easy and difficult to crack, depending on several factors.

1. Opinion columns—"think pieces"—are extremely difficult to sell, almost impossible if you are not a recognized authority of some sort. Walter Lippman was able to do it, and probably Walter Cronkite and a few others of great reputation can do it, but it's an uphill, almost hopeless battle otherwise. (That is not the same thing as true analysis columns, such as those analyzing the stock market or the latest medical findings. Even in those cases you must be able to demonstrate impressive credentials.)

2. Humor usually sells well, but it is much more difficult to write than most people believe. You will have tough acts—such as Will Rogers and Robert Benchley—to follow. You must be good—very good.

3. Something truly different and original will sell—if readers like it. And that is what it always comes down to: The readers are the final judges.

Editors buy what they think readers will like. They may be right—or wrong. Of course, they will never know without trying the column. Still, after all their years as reporters, correspondents, and newspaper editors, they "have seen it all," or believe they have. (Maybe your "new" idea is not so new, after all, to an old hand in the business!)

Syndication is usually done through an established organization, such as the King Features Syndicate or United Features, two of many syndicates. They are the professionals; they have a good idea of what is salable as a syndicated feature and what is not. They are also realists; they know that even a good idea takes time to sell to enough subscribers—newspapers—to make the proposition viable. That is why you must pay them as much as sixty percent of the selling price as their commission. And that is also why it is not easy to get them to accept you as a client.

But it is not hopeless. There is another way: Do it yourself. Be your own syndicate by selling your material directly to a number of newspapers on a syndicated basis.

Here are just a few subject areas that have potential for syndicated columns:

Advice, general

Automotive matters

Beauty and fashion

Books and periodicals

Bridge

Business

Decorating

Ecology and animals

Education

Entertainment

Food and wine

Gardening and farming

Health foods

Hobbies

Home-based businesses

Medicine and science

Music

Political scene

Religion

Retirement

Sports

Television and radio

Travel and vacations

Women and family

Bear in mind that you are up against experts, some with large reputations, as competitors. Try to specialize as much as possible—it's much easier to be a true expert in a narrow specialty than in a broad one. Try to choose an area in which you truly do have some credentials as an expert and where there are not an excessive number of competitors.

Obviously, for many of the areas, you must be a professional expert. But you could also be an "amateur expert" in areas such as wine, gardening, home-based second-income careers, and household hints. Don't underestimate the value of research to supplement—even replace—your own expert knowledge; you don't have to know it all yourself. If you are in a position to get good information on a continuing basis, you can turn that to advantage. Many journalists, for example, are not experts in their subjects, but they are expert in finding information they can use—who to call or interview, what bulletins to read.

You can easily get yourself placed on distribution lists for news releases, for example. All you need do is make up a letterhead—you can simply type it—announcing that you are a columnist, news service, publisher, or other relevant entrepreneur and request that your name be placed on the mailing list. The marketing departments of most manufacturers issue such releases, as well as full press kits, and will be happy to add your name. There are dozens of trade publications that are distributed free of charge to many people. Your local librarian will help you find lists of such periodicals.

Once you select a topic area, you will have to decide whether to specialize or generalize within that category. For example, here are some of the columnists and columns falling into the "Advice" category:

- Jean Adams: "Teen Forum"—About and for teenagers

- Dr. Joyce Brothers: Psychologist—Professional advice

- Heloise: Household hints—Solving household problems

- Joyce Lain Kennedy: Career Comer—Tips about jobs and careers

- Abigail Van Buren: Dear Abby —Advice to lovelorn and others

You must determine your audience. For the general public as an audience, you want to shoot for the daily newspapers. But if you are after a more specialized audience, such as professionals or business owners, you want to consider the trade papers. *DM News*, for example, is a tabloid for the direct-mail community, and *Target Marketing* is a smooth-paper magazine for the same audience. Both are "controlled circulation" periodicals, incidentally, which means that qualified applicants receive free subscriptions.

There are many avenues to success. An acquaintance of mine does his own syndicating. He sells a comic strip and a column on handicrafts aimed at hobbyists and homeworkers. Another man who publishes his own newsletter, offering advice and information on investments, saving money, and related subjects, also syndicates his own column on those subjects in many local newspapers.

You will probably do well to try marketing your column to weekly newspapers at first for several reasons. Editors of weekly newspapers are often easier to see and talk with, although they tend also to have rather limited budgets. If you can give your column local interest, it will be more attractive to a weekly since they are the journals of small towns, neighborhoods, and suburbia. The editor will probably be pleased to have a local writer doing a column and presumably available to discuss coverage of the column, perhaps even to accept special assignments. Certainly, the small weekly is easier to sell to than the big daily!

You don't have to limit yourself to newspapers. Consider other kinds of periodicals, including trade tabloids—many trade journals are published as "slicks" (smooth-paper magazines)—but there are many others published on newsprint as tabloids. Try also the Sunday supplements and regional slicks—many of those use syndicated material.

It's a "numbers game"—playing the percentages or probability statistics. If your column has worth and you send samples to enough editors, inevitably you will make a few sales. It will take patience and endurance, but if you persist, you will succeed. The first few sales are the hardest to make. Once you've begun, it will gradually become easier. The resources section at the end of this chapter lists the major syndicates.

Salaries

Daily newspapers pay better salaries than weekly town papers. As a rule, the larger the circulation, the better the pay. In the directories listed at the end of this chapter, you will find the names and addresses of thousands of daily newspapers.

Most journalists start with smaller dailies, then move up. Often their ultimate goal is a job with the *Boston Globe*, the *New York Times*, the *Washington Post*, *USA Today*, or the *Wall Street Journal*. These newspapers have the largest circulations and pay the highest salaries.

Of course, the top ten or twenty papers can hire a limited number of reporters and editors. So only a small fraction of reporters ever get to write for the *Times* or *Journal*.

Most reporters enjoy decent salaries, interesting work, and rewarding careers at small and medium-size papers. Staff journalists earn somewhat more than the average full-time freelance writer, but less than staff writers and communications managers in corporate positions.

The average journalist's salary in the United States is a little over $32,000 a year, but the range is wide. Many small-town reporters, even with several years of experience, earn salaries in the upper teens or low twenties. Reporters for major daily newspapers can make $40,000 to $70,000 a year or more. Some syndicated columnists, financial journalists, big-name sportswriters, and other top reporters have incomes in the six figures. Newspaper reporters, especially those at "name" papers, can supplement their income writing magazine articles or books.

Fame

Newspaper reporters usually do not become celebrities, although one of the perks of the job for many is the opportunity to meet with famous or powerful people in politics, business, and the entertainment industry.

Some newspaper reporters, such as Jimmy Breslin, do gain fame and become celebrities in their own right, though newspaper reporters never gain the star status of a rock musician or movie actor.

One unusual thing about being a reporters versus other jobs is that your name appears on the stories you write for the paper. So even though you are not a celebrity, you do gain some minor fame in your community and, if writing for a national paper, nationwide. A lot of people don't pay attention to bylines, but friends, relatives, and neighbors will probably notice your name and be suitably impressed.

But with recognition can come less desirable public notice. Some people do not like the media in general and reporters in particular. For instance, while writing this book, I called information for the phone number of the Columbia University School of Journalism. "Oh, that's where people to go learn to misrepresent the truth," the operator said cynically. While most reporters work very hard to present the news in an accurate, straightforward, unbiased manner, the unscrupulous and sometimes highly publicized practices of some reporters have contributed to a measure of discontent among the public. Others accuse the media of having a negative rather than a positive focus. But if you're someone who wants to make a difference, who wants to be part of the best of the Fourth Estate, then you'll find journalism a rewarding career.

Resources

Here are some publications that list newspapers and their editors nationwide. Publicists use these directories to place publicity releases, but they serve as excellent mailing lists for sending out resumes and cover letters when seeking a newspaper job:

Directories

Bacon's Publicity Checker. 332 S. Michigan Ave., Chicago, IL 60604. Bacon's publishes annual directories of media sources in the following categories: TV and radio, newspapers, and magazines. Bacon's will also provide pressure-sensitive mailing labels or handle the printing and mailing of your press releases for you at a reasonable rate. I use Bacon's for my clients all the time and am extremely satisfied both with the price and the results.

Editor & Publisher International Yearbook. 11 W. 19th St., New York, NY 10011. Annual directory listing the publishers and editors at more than 250,000 U.S., Canadian, and foreign newspapers. Probably the most comprehensive media directory for newspapers available.

Gebbie All-in-One Directory. Box 1000, New Paltz, NY 12561. A directory with thirty thousand listings covering newspapers, magazines, radio, and TV in a single volume. Listings are also available on computer disk or mailing labels.

The Pocket Media Guide. Media Distribution Services, 307 W. 36th St., New York, NY 10018. One of the largest full-service press release distribution services, MDS features a computerized database of 150,000 editors, reporters, and broadcasters at more than 40,000 media outlets in the United States and Canada. Call for details and a copy of the guide.

Power Media Selects. Broadcast Interview Source, 2233 Wisconsin Ave. NW, Suite 540, Washington, DC 20007. A directory with contact names, addresses, phone numbers, and profiles of more than three thousand of the most influential print and broadcast media contacts. Updated every six months. This book is selective ("influential" media), compared to Bacon's, which is comprehensive.

Major Feature Syndicates

King Features Syndicate. 235 E. 45th St., New York, NY 10017.
United Feature Syndicate. 200 Park Ave., New York, NY 10166.
Universal Press Syndicate. 490 Main Street, Kansas City, MO 64112.
New York Times Syndication Sales Corp. 130 Fifth Ave., New, York, NY
   10111.
AP Newsfeatures. 50 Rockefeller Plaza, New York, NY 10020.
United Media. 200 Park Ave., New York, NY 10166.
Newspaper Enterprise Association. 200 Park Ave., New York, NY 10166.
National News Bureau. 2019 Chancellor St., Philadelphia, PA 19103.
Los Angeles Times Syndicate. Times Mirror Square, Los Angeles, CA 90053.

CHAPTER FIVE

Careers in Advertising

The Copywriter: The Creative Side

In advertising, the copywriter is an idea person. He or she dreams up the words, the slogans, the jingles, and sometimes the visual images that appear in the ads and commercials you read and see every day.

Copywriting is creative, but it's different from other forms of creative writing. Novelists entertain; magazine writers give information; but copywriters have a tougher job: They have to write words that *sell*.

Copywriters work side by side with art directors and creative directors in the *creative department*. While account management handles the business side, the creative department is responsible for the actual writing and design of ads and commercials.

Beginning writers start as trainees, then move up to the position of junior copywriter. Junior copywriters get to write, but they handle the minor projects—product data sheets, broadsides, circulars, newspaper inserts.

Once they become full-fledged copywriters, they get to work on "major-league" print advertising and television campaigns for the agency's big accounts. The next step up for a copywriter is to become a *copy supervisor*, which involves supervising the work of a team of writers. The copy supervisor is high enough up the organizational ladder to be eligible for a vice-presidency.

A copy supervisor can go on to become an associate creative director and then the creative director, who is responsible for all creative work in the agency. The creative director supervises writers, artists, illustrators, and photographers.

There may be many creative directors in the agency. They, in turn, are supervised by a director of creative services. The director oversees major creative tasks (such as the design of a new campaign or theme) and sets the overall tone, style, and "philosophy" of the agency's creative work. The director of creative services reports directly to the agency president.

The higher up you go on this ladder, the more you'll supervise others and the less you'll write. So while the position of creative director tempts copywriters with a prestigious title, more authority, and a six-figure salary, many writers prefer to stay writers because they would rather write than manage.

Training and Background

How do you gain skill in copywriting? First, you need the skills of the general writer: the ability to write clear, concise, interesting prose. The best way to gain these skills is simply to write for your local newspaper, your college literary magazine, a trade journal, a church bulletin. Many copywriters started out as novelists, newspaper reporters, free-lance magazine writers, poets, proofreaders, or editors. Others worked as advertising managers, salespeople, or as writers for the advertising departments of manufacturers or department stores.

As you master the basics of writing, focus specifically on copywriting. Keep files of ads, articles on advertising, sales letters, and brochures that catch your eye. Study the files. What makes a given ad effective or ineffective? Pinpoint copywriting techniques that work and use them in your own writing.

Put together a notebook of your own copy samples. At first, these will be "speculative" ads: ads you've written on your own rather than for a real client. Once you get some experience, you can add clippings of your published ads to the book. The book is your portfolio—a collection of your copywriting samples that demonstrates your ability to prospective employers.

One quick way of building a portfolio is to create new ads for existing products. Paste published ads for these products on the left-hand pages of your book. Rewrite the published ads to make them better, and put your improved versions on the facing right-hand pages. This before-and-after format can make a dramatic presentation of your ability to outdo the pros.

Every copywriter needs a portfolio. One that contains published ads is best, but many beginners have gained their first job by showing a portfolio of speculative ads.

Although you should look neat, clean, and professional on your job interview, appearance on the job is not as important for the writer as it is for the account executive. In many creative departments, artists and writers wear casual clothes (jeans, sports shirts, tennis shoes) and save their single three-piece suit for the occasional client meeting. "If you're a writer or artist, you can be more crazy," complains one account executive. "They call it 'creative.'"

However, a business suit is still the appropriate attire for job interviews. Once you get the position, you'll quickly catch on to the agency's dress code.

A broad liberal arts education is the best training for copywriters because their job is to combine specific product knowledge with general knowledge of people, places, events, and the world at large to come up with advertisements that sell the product by making it relevant to the consumer's life. The liberal arts allow students to soak up knowledge in such varied and useful fields as creative writing, journalism, poetry, human relations, management, marketing, economics, psychology, and history—all recommended fare for aspiring copywriters.

Specific courses in copywriting can also be valuable, depending on the teacher. Look for courses where the teacher has had professional copywriting experience; you can only learn this skill from someone who knows the field. By doing all the homework assignments, you can build a portfolio of copy to present to prospective employers. Many students have landed copywriting jobs after completing such courses and putting together sample books of their assignments.

Education doesn't end with college, however. The best copywriters continue to be students throughout their lives and are interested in practically everything. They read books, trade journals, magazines, newspapers; see plays and films; visit galleries, museums, historical sites; keep extensive clipping files of information on all sorts of subjects. They also read popular magazines and watch television to see what other advertisers are doing and to keep up with the tastes of the general public.

For decades, copywriters have studied what works and what doesn't work in advertising, and many have written books describing their discoveries and techniques. Reading books on advertising and copywriting can give you in a few hours what it took these people decades to learn.

In particular, read any of the books by David Ogilvy, John Caples, Rosser Reeves, Claude Hopkins, or James Webb Young. Other books of interest may be found in the bibliography at the end of this chapter.

Copywriters also study people—how they behave; what they do; what they look like; what they eat, wear, and buy. As a copywriter, every person you meet is a potential source of information for your next campaign, and you're always listening to what people say, hoping to capture a comment that could turn into a great slogan or headline.

Many writers prefer to lead solitary lives, hunched over the typewriter banging out the Great American Novel. But the ad agency copywriter is a team player, working closely with account executives, art directors, and creative directors. "Advertising isn't a business for loners, for prima donnas, and I wish that more people...would understand this," writes advertising consultant Whit Hobbs in *Adweek*. "This is a very tough, complicated business, and again and again it has been proved that the more effectively people work together to create advertising, the more successful the advertising."

Although it's unusual for agencies to offer training programs for copywriters, many big agencies will hire novices and train them informally. If you can't get in as a copywriter, you can start as a secretary or administrative assistant. But be warned: That's a tough route to take, and the chances of your actually moving up to a copywriter's position are slim. Most agencies want their secretaries to remain secretaries; only a few will give secretaries the opportunity to write copy part-time and then advance to a full-time copywriting job. The majority of agencies prefer to hire writers from outside the agency, and they rarely promote clerical staff.

Money

Copywriting can be a well-paying profession. Your starting salary may be low, but after a few years you'll be taking home respectable (if not astronomical) paychecks. And if you become a superstar, your salary could soar into the mid-six figures, exceeding the paychecks of many corporate presidents and CEOs.

According to Adweek's "1994 Annual Salary Survey," the median 1994 salary for copywriters was $48,300. The average copywriter in the top 10 percent earned $61,200. The survey also pinpointed some interesting trends:

- Account executives (AEs) start at higher salaries than copywriters, but senior copywriters usually make more than account executives of equal experience.

- The bigger the agency or account, the more the account executive, copywriter, or creative director makes. An account executive at a $150-million agency earns, on average, one-third more than his or her counterpart at a $5-million agency.

- *Writers* and *AEs* are paid the most in East and West Coast agencies, the least in the Midwest and the South.

- The best-paid people in the advertising industry are not AEs or writers but *independent (free-lance) television directors*. A typical director's fee ranges from $7,500 to $20,000 for one day's shooting; top directors—such as Bob Giraldi and Joe Sedelmaier—earn more than a million dollars a year. These directors are hired by various agencies to direct commercials on a per-project basis.

- On the agency side, top *creative directors* can earn $300,000 to $400,000 a year and more. Top account-management salaries, while in the six figures, can't match this.

Dick Wasserman, a vice-president at Needham, Harper & Steers, wrote up the results of his own salary survey in an article in *Advertising Age*. To get his data, Wasserman went to Jerry Kindman, a New York CPA who, along with his two partners, handles the tax returns of some three thousand advertising people each year. Two-thirds of his clients are writers or artists, and one-third are account executives.

Kindman compiled average salary figures for his copywriter clients according to the number of years they'd spent in the business:

Experience	Annual salary
Beginners	$11,000–$15,000
1–2 years	$15,000–$25,000
3–4 years	$18,000–$30,000
5–7 years	$25,000–$35,000
7–10 years	$35,000–$50,000
10–15 years	$40,000–$80,000
15–25 years	$50,000–$200,000

Wasserman drew a few interesting conclusions from Kindman's figures and from the results of other surveys he made:

- To move beyond the $40,000–$60,000 annual salary, a copywriter must have success in writing commercials as well as print advertising. A reel (sample film reel or videotape) of five good commercials is a must for copywriters who want to move up in the world of big-agency advertising.

- Once they get beyond the beginner level, copywriters earn more than AEs.

- Although agencies don't come right out and say it, they do prefer to hire younger people. Kindman said he couldn't recall having a client over fifty. The agency business is oriented toward youth and is a difficult job market for older people looking to begin a new career.

- High salaries go to copywriters and creative directors who are willing to work in branch offices outside New York or on certain types of accounts that no one else wants to handle (such as cigarettes).

For copywriters, the pay is good, the business exciting, the job challenging and rewarding. Best of all, it doesn't take highly specialized training, skill, or technical knowledge to break in.

Getting Started

Although many advertising greats never got past high school, nowadays an undergraduate degree is needed to land most account-management or copywriting jobs. A recent survey of three hundred advertising professionals showed that three-quarters had a bachelor's degree or higher.

Most advertising executives recommend that aspiring writers, whatever their major, take a good mix of courses in English literature and composition, journalism, speech, business administration, math, social sciences, economics, psychology, accounting, marketing, and advertising. The best preparation is to blend this academic training with job experience in a career allied with or related to advertising—sales, media, print production, journalism, photography.

However, advertising is gaining popularity as a major course of study in its own right. Michigan State University, with 1,208 students and twelve full-time professors, has one of the largest degree programs in advertising. The course of study includes accounting, marketing, math, computer science, writing, psychology, sociology, media planning, consumer behavior, management, and research. In addition, the senior class is divided into "agencies" that compete for a real-life account and develop a campaign that the company will use. Other schools with advertising programs include Texas Tech University, the University of Alabama, Louisiana State University, the University of Oregon, and Boston University.

Be aware that many advertising executives are skeptical of academia's ability to prepare students for life in the "real world" of advertising. So while a college education in advertising may have a lot to offer, it won't necessarily make you a more attractive candidate to potential employers.

In addition to these academic programs, several of the top agencies have formal in-house training programs for account management, media, art, copywriting, and market research. Unfortunately, there are a limited number of openings in these programs; a survey of the largest twenty agencies revealed that twelve have formal training programs for which, all together, they hire only 145 new trainees each year.

When you've completed your basic training and are ready to offer yourself to the working world, you'll need to write a great resume and a sharp cover letter. Remember, there are hundreds (maybe thousands) of people like you competing for the job you want. Sure, you're bright, well educated, and willing to work hard. But they are, too. And many are far more experienced.

So you need a sharp, no-nonsense resume and a hard-selling cover letter to set you apart from the crowd.

This isn't as awesome a task as it sounds. One personnel director reports that of the eight thousand resumes he receives each year, two-thirds contain typos, spelling mistakes, or grammatical errors. So if you proofread your resume thoroughly and have a few other people take a look at it, you're already ahead of two-thirds of the pack!

Although having a letter-perfect resume is important, it's not enough to land you a job interview. You also need a persuasive cover letter to convince the prospective employer to see you.

In an article for *Free Enterprise* magazine, copywriter Don Hauptman stresses the need to use "tailored letters"—individual letters tailored to the particular agency or job advertised. "The tailored letter focuses on the *specifics* of the position in question," says Hauptman. "It tells what the applicant can do for the employer."

Such a letter is far more effective than using a form letter or just popping your resume in the mail with no cover letter. According to a study by the California Employment Development Department, 46 percent of tailored letters result in job interviews, as opposed to only 2 percent of resumes mailed without cover letters.

Hauptman observes that the biggest fault of most cover letters is their failure to address the needs and interests of the employer, or the job description, qualifications, and responsibilities as stated in the help-wanted ad. He cites as an example the experience of the head of a high-tech firm who advertised for an administrative assistant in the local paper. Of two hundred replies he received, only four letters even alluded to the qualifications and duties outlined in the ad!

The cover letter—especially one sent to a busy creative director or agency president—should sell you to the agency. Be aggressive. You should know you're the best candidate for the job; let the reader know it, too. You should end the letter by promising to follow up with a phone call in a week or so to set up an appointment.

Take this situation, for example: The advertising manager of an industrial firm wanted to write copy for a big ad agency. But the ad agency's help-wanted ad strictly stated, "We will only consider copywriters with agency experience—no others need apply."

The ad manager had no agency experience and was infuriated by this bit of snobbery. His powerful letter, reprinted below, turned his lack of experience into an asset and resulted in a job interview:

Dear Creative Director:

Your *Adweek* classified says you're looking for a copywriter with agency experience.

Why?

I'm a writer on the client side. The product managers I work for aren't interested in slick, pretty ads that win creative awards. They demand (and I give them) copy and concepts that generate leads, create awareness, and increase sales.

Rather than build a portfolio of splashy four-color advertisements, I've built campaigns that achieve marketing objectives within set budgets.

Now, the average agency copywriter may write more ads than I do. But my book will show you that I do first-rate work. And if that's not enough, I challenge you to try me out on a few assignments and see if I don't top every agency-experienced writer that applies for this position.

Sincerely,

Joe Doakes

Of course, a compelling cover letter is no guarantee of an interview. Mail-order companies are happy to get one or two orders for every hundred direct-mail packages they send out; as a job seeker, you can expect similar results. You're doing great if you get a handful of "yes, come in and see us" calls in response to a mailing of several dozen letters.

Don't be discouraged by this low response rate; it only takes one good response to result in a job. Instead, be persistent. Keep writing letters, and you'll eventually get a response and some interviews.

When you go on interviews, your style in person should match that of your letters—professional and polite, but aggressive and ready to sell. Be punctual. Look like a businessperson: Wear a suit; be clean and neat; if you're a man, keep your hair short. Do a little research about the agency—its size, major clients, and track record—before the interview.

Copywriters, of course, must bring their portfolios. Account executives can bring whatever they think will best show their qualifications—marketing plans they've written, a portfolio of campaigns they've supervised, market research studies they've conducted, even letters of praise from happy clients.

Don't be a wallflower. Ask the interviewer a lot of questions about his or her agency and the help they need in the department you'd want to work in. And tell the interviewer why you're the right person for the job.

Always send a thank-you note after every interview. So few people do this that it really sets you apart from the crowd and can turn a maybe into a yes.

If you don't get the job, try to analyze why. Listen to the creative director's critique of your portfolio or the account supervisor's analysis of your background and the experience you lack. If you hear the same comments from a number of different interviewers, a change might be in order. Perhaps you need to improve your copywriting samples, or get more experience, or take a couple of courses. Be realistic about whether you are qualified for the job you seek.

On the other hand, don't be disappointed when the first few interviews don't result in a job offer. We've talked to beginning agency people who said it took them a year or more to get their first job! Even an experienced writer can spend two to six months on the street before finding an agency whose needs fit his or her experience.

So don't despair. Be patient, and if you were meant to work in advertising, you will get that job. However, many people find that the competitive, frantic pace is not for them and that they would be happier in another type of business or writing job.

Recognize, too, that the advertising business is one where contacts make a difference; it helps if you have a friend or relative in a position of authority at a major agency. If you're fortunate enough to have such a contact, take full advantage of it.

Moving Up

Some industries frown upon job-hopping. But not so advertising. A lot of people in the business—account executives, creative directors, even headhunters and agency heads—actually encourage job-hopping in the early years of a career because it gives you a broad range of experience and boosts your salary.

A study conducted by the 4A's, an industry association, showed a 31 percent annual turnover rate in advertising. Judd Falk, an executive search firm, estimated the turnover rate to be between 30 and 35 percent.

In its "Adweek Salary Survey," *Adweek* even outlined a career path designed to make your job-hopping more productive and profitable. The article recommends you start in a big agency to get training and earn the most money you can at the entry-level and junior positions. After you've soaked up an education at the big agency's expense, move to a smaller agency. When you make this move, you'll get a more senior position, more money, and more managerial experience.

If the small agency doesn't grow, switch back to a big agency—this time at the level of account supervisor, creative director, or department head. Look for a big increase in salary when you do.

This sounds logical and may work for some people. In truth, however, there is no surefire formula for success. You have to follow your instincts and grab opportunities as they arise.

It *is* true that strategically shifting from big agency to small agency and back can hasten your progress up the managerial and salary ladders. Here are a few observations to help you shift at the right time and to the right place:

- Big agencies offer many paths for career advancement, but you can be quickly dead-ended at a small agency. "Getting a good position with a small agency is no big deal," said one former small-agency writer. "After all, if you take a job with a five-man agency, you're already in the number-five spot the day you start. And the owner isn't likely to ever let you get to number one."

- The biggest advantage of working for a small agency is that you'll get to handle a broader range of tasks. Small agencies can't afford to hire a specialist for every job, so their employees wear many different hats. A copywriter, for example, might also meet with the client, help plan the advertising schedule, supervise photographers and artists, and even get involved with media buying and printing. This education will be valuable to you later on; for instance, it will give you an understanding of how other departments work when you take a more specialized job at a big agency.

- Most small agencies concentrate on print advertising. And most creative directors look for a solid foundation in print before they'll train you in television. So by working at a small agency, you can quickly build a portfolio of good-quality print ads. You'll also learn to write brochures, catalogs, and direct-mail pieces—skills that may help you get a job with a larger agency.

- For the most part, only the big agencies have the money, resources, and manpower to service major national accounts. You need to work on these accounts if you want to gain prestige and status in the advertising community.

- With some exceptions, only the major agencies do any substantial work in television. You need television experience to break out of the $50,000-a-year mold and earn the top salaries.

- The small-agency job market is less competitive. Most people would rather work at big agencies on big accounts. Smaller agencies often have trouble attracting and holding on to talented writers, artists, account executives, and media people. So if the big-agency game is unpalatable, you can still find happiness—albeit with less money and status—at one of the thousands of fine small agencies operating throughout the United States. The choice is up to you.

Required Reading for Aspiring Copywriters

Books

Here are some books you can read to dig deeper into the advertising business. The list includes a mix of textbooks, how-to books, autobiographies, memoirs, and history books. Enjoy!

Arlen, Michael J. *Thirty Seconds*. New York: Farrar, Straus & Giroux, 1980. Chronicles the making of one of the thirty-second commercials in AT&T's "Reach out and touch someone" campaign. An entertaining inside look at the world of big-league advertising.

Bly, Robert W. *The Copywriter's Handbook: A Step-by-Step Guide to Writing Copy That Sells*. New York: Dodd, Mead, 1985. A guide to writing effective ad copy, plus advice on career opportunities in copywriting.

Caples, John. *How to Make Your Advertising Make Money*. Englewood Cliffs, N.J.: Prentice-Hall, 1983. Caples, master of the hard sell, reveals secrets and techniques for creating advertising campaigns that get results.

Cummings, Barton A. *The Benevolent Dictators: Interviews with Eighteen Ad Agency Greats*. Chicago: Crain Books, 1984. Insights into the lives of eighteen industry leaders and how they ran their great agencies.

Dunn, S. W., and A. M. Barban. *Advertising: Its Role in Modern Marketing*. Hinsdale, IL: The Dryden Press, 1978. A readable textbook that presents a comprehensive overview of the advertising business.

Eicoff, Alvin. *Or Your Money Back*. New York: Crown, 1982. Eicoff is one of the masters of the late-night mail-order TV commercial.

Periodicals

Like any business professional, copywriters should keep up-to-date by reading magazines in their field. There are dozens of excellent publications covering various areas of advertising, sales, and marketing. Here, I list twelve I've found useful. Some I subscribe to; others I read on a hit-or-miss basis. All will help you learn more about copywriting in particular and advertising in general.

Ad Day/U.S.A., 49 E. 21st St., New York, NY 10010. *Ad Day* is a weekly newsletter on what's happening in the advertising business. It reports on account changes, new ad campaigns, and who's moving where and is useful for its late-breaking news.

Ad Forum, 18 E. 53rd St., New York, NY 10022. This monthly magazine is aimed at the marketing manager who works for a consumer company. Much of the editorial content focuses on creating, managing, and measuring print and broadcast advertising campaigns aimed at a mass audience.

Advertising Age, 740 N. Rush St., Chicago, IL 60611. This twice-weekly news magazine is one of the two top industry publications (the other being *Adweek*). *Advertising Age* contains in-depth coverage of newsworthy events in advertising; the midweek edition features a special "magazine section" that focuses on a specific area of advertising. Recent magazine sections have profiled computer, retail, direct response, grocery, and fashion advertising.

Adweek, 49 E. 21st St., New York, NY 10010. *Adweek* is *Advertising Age*'s main competitor. *Adweek* is smaller, slimmer, more compact than *Ad Age*, and it comes out only once a week. (To make up for this, *Adweek* recently purchased *Ad Day*, which it publishes on Thursdays to compete with *Ad Age*'s Thursday edition.) *Adweek* offers readers a blend of news, features, how-to articles, and lively columns. I subscribe to both magazines but prefer *Adweek* for its concise format that lets me get the news in less time.

Business Marketing, 220 E. 42nd St., New York, NY 10017. *Business Marketing* covers advertising, sales, and marketing of products and services sold to business and industry. It's a "must-read" for industrial, high-tech, medical, and financial copywriters. *Business Marketing*'s editorial content is heavy on long feature articles—both "how-to" articles and analytical pieces. Published monthly.

Direct Marketing, 224 Seventh St., Garden City, NY 11530. *Direct Marketing* is for readers involved in direct-response marketing—direct mail, mail order, telemarketing. Every issue is loaded with "how-to" articles on various facets of copywriting. I subscribe to *Direct Marketing* and recommend it even if you're not involved in direct mail or mail order. Published monthly.

DM News, 19 W. 21st St., New York, NY 10010. A newspaper-style tabloid. Coverage is similar to *Direct Marketing*, but articles are briefer and more oriented toward late-breaking news rather than general information. *DM News* also publishes several helpful how-to articles in each issue. Published twice a month.

Madison Avenue, 140 Riverside Dr., New York, NY 10024. As the name implies, *Madison Avenue* is for people involved in the world of big-agency, big-account advertising. It's a well written, attractively designed magazine with many useful articles. Published monthly.

Marketing Communications, 228 E. 45th St., New York, NY 10017. A down-to-earth, informative publication, primarily for advertising professionals involved in retail advertising. Published monthly.

Public Relations Journal, 33 Irving Pl., New York, NY 10003. This is the official monthly magazine of the Public Relations Society of America for public relations professionals. Copywriters just getting into public relations can learn a lot from this magazine on how to write material that editors will read and publish.

Sales and Marketing Management, 633 Third Ave., New York, NY 10017. A monthly magazine for sales managers and marketing managers, *Sales and Marketing Management* runs informative articles on all facets of marketing—including advertising. Most of the articles are brief and instructive.

Target Marketing, 401 N. Broad St., Philadelphia, PA 19108. Deals primarily with the mailing-list aspect of direct marketing. It will give copywriters a good overview of direct marketing as well as specific tips on creative direct mail that works. Published monthly.

CHAPTER SIX

Public Relations

With public sentiment, nothing can fail. Without it, nothing can succeed.
—ABRAHAM LINCOLN

We have bad news and good news about the field of public relations. Briefly, the bad news first.

Ever since the days of P.T. Barnum, publicity, also known as "public relations," has had a seedy connotation. Public relations (PR) people are derogatorily called "flacks" and have been portrayed in countless books and films as fawning, exploitative, and insensitive.

The field of public relations is not for applause-seekers. The best PR is invisible, and the best PR people stay behind the scenes.

Public relations is a detail-oriented, high-pressure career. It is known as a thankless profession. If you don't produce results, you're fired; if you do produce results, you don't always get full credit.

Now, the good news:

The field of public relations is growing rapidly, and there are numerous opportunities to find entry-level positions. The field is exciting because you are dealing with the media as well as the public. There's often an opportunity to travel, earn a respectable salary, and use your mind in a variety of ways. Public relations is a challenge to people with liberal arts backgrounds. It appreciates skills in writing.

Public Relations Defined

Just what is "public relations," and how does it differ from advertising? Public relations works toward gaining public awareness of a product or service via the editorial side of the media to achieve specific goals.

While advertising people create advertisements and commercials that are paid for by sponsors, public relations people attempt to help people or organizations reach their publics in a more indirect way. A film star's publicist, for example, might suggest that the star appear as a guest on a talk show. The resulting interview would almost surely mention the star's upcoming projects.

If all of the public relations agencies of the United States were to shut their doors tomorrow, most radio and talk shows, as well as many newspapers and magazines, would soon have to follow suit. Why? Because the American media—including NBC's "The Tonight Show," the *Wall Street Journal,* and the major magazines—depend upon publicity releases to keep them abreast of what is going on. True, these organizations have their own staffs to help assemble material for their shows and publications, but public relations firms form a surprisingly large information lobby. In fact, they provide many of the "news" stories we see and read every day.

There are more than three thousand bona fide public relations firms in the United States, and there are countless other "vest-pocket" firms that are run from the homes of individuals.

The opportunities in public relations are vast because virtually every store, company, restaurant, and celebrity can use publicity to help gain public awareness and, by so doing, make more money for themselves. A restaurant that puts its name on matches and ashtrays is engaging in a form of promotion; so is a consultant who sends Christmas cards to potential clients. So is an art gallery dealer or party-goods store owner who puts out a newsletter. All of these are examples of publicity or promotion, not advertising.

On a grander scale, companies and public organizations (e.g., the National Rifle Association, the Dairy Association) often spend millions of dollars to win public acceptance, to introduce new products, and to gain media coverage. Political candidates must weigh the public-relations impact of practically every stand they take, every group they address, and every place they visit. Doctors, dentists, and dietitians often leave brochures about health scattered throughout their lobbies because it's good promotion.

Public relations can increase sales either directly or indirectly. An example of direct impact is the sending of press releases for a new product or a new use for an old product. An example of indirect public relations would be a food company's sending of recipes that include its product as an ingredient to food editors. These recipes may even end up in feature stories that mention the company's product. This indirectness gives public relations its reputation for nebulousness. The amount of good will or sales generated by a promotional campaign is often difficult, if not impossible, to measure.

Sometimes the best public relations involves checking or limiting the damage of negative media exposure. When a few Extra-Strength Tylenol capsules in Chicago were found to contain cyanide, the Johnson & Johnson Company limited the damage done to the product's image by acting with admirable speed, forthrightness, and savvy. They instantly acknowledged the problem and initiated a recall of the product long before the Food and Drug Administration could even suggest it. They were also accessible to the press, and they helped in the investigation. The recall cost Johnson & Johnson more than $100 million, but it upheld the company's reputation. A great deal of credit goes to the Johnson & Johnson public relations people who, through quick thinking and a respect for the intelligence of the American public, managed to avert what could have been a publicity disaster. The public relations effort was internal as well as external. Employees of McNeil Consumer Products Company, the Johnson & Johnson unit responsible for Tylenol, began sporting buttons with a thumbs-up design and the words "We're Coming Back."

Public relations is an exciting field because it challenges people to think of ways in which products and services can gain media attention. If, however, public relations people fall into the habit of lying, playing down the negative, or avoiding painful issues, they can create bad publicity. When Rely Tampons were shown to be associated with Toxic Shock Syndrome, the manufacturer of Rely was reluctant to acknowledge the problem. That reluctance alone practically destroyed the brand because it destroyed the product's credibility. To be good at public relations, you must fight the human tendency to deny responsibility.

Enjoying public relations and promotion requires accepting the fact that your job is to seize opportunities to help the public see a product or service the way you see it or the way your client sees it. The field is not for shy people; it's for assertive people who are not troubled by rejection. It may involve using everything from press releases, interviews, press conferences, direct mail, and flyers to T-shirts, buttons, pens, toys, and telephone calls to help influence people to take notice of your service or product.

There are approximately 120,000 people in the public relations field, one-quarter of them women. One-half of all people in public relations work in New York City; Washington, D.C.; Chicago; and Los Angeles.

Rewards and Opportunities

College graduates beginning in public relations start at between $20,000 and $27,000 a year. The average salary for experienced PR people is about $45,000 a year. Salaries are highest in the Northeast and lowest in the South.

Those entering the field of public relations have never had such a wide variety of opportunities. Many veer toward consumer public relations, where they publicize products and services used by consumers: books, plays, food, health and beauty aids, travel, appliances, and restaurants. Less known, but equally important, are trade and industrial public relations, which involves publicity aimed at business people, including store owners, doctors, and distributors.

The rapidly expanding health field offers public relations opportunities in hospitals, pharmaceutical companies, and medical associations. Another growth area, according to one vice-president of public relations for a major corporation, is human resources planning, which used to be employee communications. Public policy planning, also a growing area, requires some type of government experience. There are also emerging public relations opportunities in the fields of ecology, finance, economic education, and government regulation.

In addition to these choices, the person entering public relations must decide whether to work in a corporate communications office or in a public relations agency. Public relations professionals can prosper within an agency, or they can make a home for themselves in nonprofit organizations, hospitals, or foundations, as well as governmental public interest groups (e.g. Common Cause), corporations, and trade associations. A bright newcomer with top writing and presentation skills can succeed in any of these areas.

What It Takes

We have mentioned that public relations, while exciting, is also detail oriented. Although it attracts many liberal arts types, it often requires the meticulousness of an engineer. Here is a run-down of the most important skills and abilities you'll need to succeed in public relations:

1. *Define problems.* The ability to understand a problem and find ways of solving it is a key to success in public relations. Sometimes, the problem can't be solved, but it can be alleviated. For example, when the telephone company's installers went on strike, there was a lot of negative publicity about all of the inconvenience being caused. A smart PR person was hired and the negative publicity soon eased up. Why? Because the PR person made sure that important media figures were able to get their phones installed and serviced. Similarly, during the Vietnam War, campus unrest over the draft was alleviated by the development of a lottery system—a brilliant public relations feat. The war went on, but the campuses became much quieter.

2. *Think logically.* Just as computer programmers think logically when they create "flow charts," a PR person must plan projects, such as press parties, interviews, exhibits, and direct-mail programs, by thinking of each step of the project. Once a project has been conceived, the nuts-and-bolts work begins; that means deciding what has to be done by when, working backwards from the final target date so that you can meet deadlines. An experienced PR professional knows that unforeseen delays are likely to slow down any project, and therefore plans must be made that allow for human frailty.

3. *Writing and editing.* These allied skills are crucial to anyone who works in public relations. Sensitivity to good writing

and an ability to recognize and edit bad writing will make your written work stand out. These skills will allow you to progress from writing one-page press releases to elaborate brochures, booklets, feature stories, and press kits.

4. *Creativity.* This often overused word refers to the ability to view an old problem with fresh eyes. It's knowing the rules plus seeing beyond them.

5. A *mind for detail.* There are dozens of details involved in the simplest public relations project. Even the distribution of a press release requires writing, rewriting, editing, printing, stapling, folding, inserting, and mailing. You must buy or create a mailing list, keep it updated constantly, and purchase envelopes. You need to know procedures for getting a bulk mail permit, and you have to buy postage and address the envelopes. By the time you get to planning a press party for five hundred people, the details become almost an endless stream, right up to checking to see if the microphones are working and whether or not the bartender has enough club soda.

6. *Presentation and interpersonal skills.* Your skills should involve a wide range of communication talents that cover everything from selling your ideas at a meeting or over cocktails to giving a formal speech at a press conference, trade show, or press party.

7. *Tenacity.* Publicists who are trying to place stories in the media must be tenacious or they will quickly become discouraged. One placement may require weeks of effort. Dozens of newspapers or radio stations say "No" before one says "Yes." You must recognize that; by sticking to it, you will probably make the placement. In short, you must have the optimism of a salesperson and the persistence of a freelance writer.

8. *Ability to work with the press and with management.* Working with managers is different from working with the press, and you must be able to switch "languages" with ease. Managers care about the bottom line; editors and reporters care about news. Each sees the publicist through different eyes, and you must be what both need.

9. *Knowledge of the media.* By understanding the media, you can learn how to best shape your communications. If you know that a particular magazine has a three-month lead-time, you can immediately determine whether a story that's "hot" is even worth sending over. Perhaps that item should go to a daily newspaper. A knowledge of deadlines will also help you determine which media may be right for which press releases. By dealing with journalists, and by taking courses in journalism, you'll soon become accustomed to seeing your stories as an editor sees them. You'll know how a release should look, and you'll learn to phrase it to rivet the editor's attention. When dealing with television, you'll automatically think of your client's story in visual terms. Certain topics—exercise, cooking, games, fashion—are "naturals" for television, while others—books, restaurants, and music—are ideal for radio.

10. *Integrity.* There is no substitute for integrity and reliability. You can't afford to lie to the press—they'll never forgive you. If you try to create a smokescreen, or simply make up facts as you go along, you'll lose your credibility and never regain it. When a reporter asks you if the president of your company just awarded himself a $100,000 bonus, and you know he did, you'd better admit the truth or at least say that you'll look into it. Denying the truth or making puffed-up claims about your product will almost always come back to haunt you.

11. *Acknowledgment of what you know and what you don't know.* A good manager knows when and how to delegate authority. If you're weak on the graphics end of the business, learn how to communicate with designers and then trust them to be competent in their area. You should gain enough knowledge to know just how far a printer, designer, or copywriter should be trusted. But, once you decide to trust them, don't let your ego get in the way of their creativity.

Training

These skills and abilities can be acquired through a blend of college studies and real-world experience. More than 100 colleges and 25 graduate schools offer degree programs or special accreditation in public relations, which is usually administered by the journalism or communications department. In addition, more than 250 colleges offer at least one course in the field. Some typical courses included organizational communication, public relations management, and public relations theory and techniques.

Taking college-level courses in public relations is important, but so is a general liberal arts background. Get a course or two in nonfiction writing under your belt and then major in a discipline such as economics, psychology, nutrition, or computer sciences. A degree in journalism is helpful, but only if it doesn't preclude your taking other enriching courses in a variety of fields. College is a place to learn how to think. Later, you can apply these skills to public relations through an internship program or on your first job in the field.

A college education is only the beginning. To do well in public relations takes an assertive, outgoing person. It takes a knowledge of business and a knowledge of important issues. It also takes reliability and loyalty. Don't worry about not understanding all the minutiae of printing or design. You'll have your whole career to pick up the thousands of details you'll need to round out your public relations education.

Getting Started

Since the essence of public relations is communication, your resume, cover letter, and interpersonal style must display the crispness, clarity, and conciseness of the promotional material you write.

There is no room in this field for hackneyed cover letters, all-purpose resumes, or insubstantial portfolios. Everything you show to a potential employer must be oriented to that employer's specific needs. This may mean that you won't be able to send out resumes and cover letters en masse, but it also means that you'll probably get more serious consideration at those organizations that receive your material.

The ideal public relations resume describes what you've done—direct mail, press releases, photography, art direction, media contact—and it also zeros in on the results. For example, if you've written and distributed a release about a product or service, tell the reader how many media pick-ups the release received. If you were responsible for a direct-mail campaign, give your response rate. In other words, write a resume that is a functional summary of what you've done and the positive results your work produced.

If you are coming straight from college, the same principle still holds true. Did you work on the school paper? If so, how did you leave your mark? Perhaps you were responsible for instituting a column on restaurants. Perhaps you helped create a direct-mail campaign that increased circulation by 25 percent. In short, be specific; show a potential employer that your influence was felt. Furthermore, be brief. Use bullets to summarize technical information and to focus on your accomplishments. Whatever you do, don't go overboard and say that you did things when, in fact, you didn't.

Prepare a draft of your resume and then show it to people who are used to looking at and evaluating resumes. You might, for instance, show it to people in the college placement office. You might also take a copy by the school's public affairs office. After all, they are public relations professionals, and they can give you insight into how PR people will view what you've written.

After writing and rewriting your resume, get it professionally desktop published and offset printed. In public relations, more than any other field, neatness counts. No typos, strike-overs, or narrow margins are allowed.

The cover letter should be individualized. Address it to the needs of a specific employer. Form letters are out; they'll make you look foolish. Here's an example of a cover letter written to a small public relations company in New York:

Dear Mr. Smith:

I am interested in interviewing for a position with your company.

My career focus is primarily in 35-mm slide presentations, although I have a varied graphics background. My greatest strength lies in my ability to communicate with coworkers and clients.

I have a solid audiovisual foundation. At this time, my goal is to pursue this rapidly expanding communications field.

Your consideration is greatly appreciated. I would welcome the opportunity of an interview with you to tell you more about myself and will take the liberty of calling you in a week or so.

Sincerely yours,

John Doe

At first glance, this cover letter seems to do the job, but a closer inspection shows that it lacks care. The most important problem is that this letter was written to a one-man public relations company, hardly the type that would do this type of specialized hiring. It is obviously a form letter and was probably sent to dozens of public relations agencies simultaneously.

The letter is writer oriented, not reader oriented. Good letters focus on the needs of the reader, not the writer. Try to imagine what the reader needs to know, rather than simply parading a list of your skills in front of her. Cover letters, as with almost every other element of selling, require that you take what you have to say and put it into a format that conforms to what your reader wishes to read.

Finally, the letter exhibits blandness and a tendency toward cliché. The sentence, "My greatest strength lies in my ability to communicate with coworkers and clients" is too weak to have any impact. The phrase, "Your consideration is greatly appreciated" is also weak, thanking the reader for something he or she has yet to do.

Another cover letter, which was sent after a brief conversation with the head of another one-man public relations shop, reads:

Dear Charles,

I have enclosed my resume as we discussed a while ago. I hope we will be able to work with each other in the near future.

Thank you for your consideration.

This letter presents several problems. The salutation, "Dear Charles," is overly informal. The first sentence is awkward and imprecise (enclosing a resume was probably not the subject of the discussion). The next sentence contains a grammatical error ("each other") and is so vague as to have no meaning. The last sentence is also too indefinite. Exactly what does the writer want? Does he want an interview? Will he call? Does he want full- or part-time work? Or does he want to be kept in mind for free-lance projects?

By the way, this letter was followed up with a phone call two months after it was sent. Such a delay is simply foolish. By that time, the reader has forgotten the letter. When you've written a letter, follow up within one or two weeks, not when the mood strikes or when you discover that you are desperate for work.

Now, let's take a look at two very focused cover letters. The first is from a free-lancer looking for occasional work, and the second is from a professional who is looking for full-time employment:

Dear Mr. Smith,

In every public relations agency there are times when the workload builds until the services of a free-lancer who can step in and "do" are desperately needed. When those times occur at your firm, I can help.

I have had a broad base of public relations experience, including promotion, media placement, fund-raising, program development, special events, and community programs.

I have taken ideas from their inception, coordinated the various aspects to bring the ideas into being, and produced the desired programs. This background provides me with unique experience which can be useful to your agency.

Enclosed is a flyer that outlines my experience and accomplishments. I would appreciate the opportunity to show you samples of my work and discuss how I could be of service to your firm.

Sincerely,

John Doe

This letter is not perfect—but it is pretty good. It has a "you" orientation that puts the emphasis on the reader's needs. Paragraph three is a bit vague, and paragraph four is one, long run-on sentence, but basically the letter works. The next letter works even better because it is specific and functional, thus highlighting the resume enclosed with it:

Dear Mr. Stevens,

As vice-president of an audiovisual production company, I expanded the Acme, Incorporated, account from $5,000 to $65,000 per year. I also brought in Procter and Gamble, New York Telephone, Prime Computers and Dean Witter.

If you are looking for someone with strong communications sales experience, you just found him. Let me mention some specific accomplishments:

- Developed seventeen new accounts, which generated $425,000 in total income
- Increased my total billing 40 percent each year for three years
- Initiated an aggressive marketing campaign to three trade shows per year, generating at least one new client for each show.

With eight years of experience in all aspects of sales and production, I believe I can generate sales and profits for your company.

If the timing is right, I would be happy to meet with you at your convenience.

Sincerely,

John Doe

This is a good letter, but ultimately unsuccessful because it was sent to a one-person shop that could never be in the position of hiring this type of specialist. It is specific and clear, although it has not been individualized to the reader's needs; therefore, it comes off as a form letter.

Let's summarize a few key points about the writing of cover letters:

1. Decide what the employer is looking for before you write a letter. Don't waste time and postage on shops that would not be in the market for what you do.

2. Be honest about your experience. Don't be afraid to admit that your background isn't a perfect match for a particular job. Stress other work you've done that might compensate for it.

3. Keep copies of all your cover letters and the ads you respond to. This helps you keep track of the salary range you've quoted and the particular job requirements of each organization. You may get a response to your cover letter months after you've sent it.

4. Name a salary range. The low side should be compatible with the salary being offered. By doing this, you'll be able to negotiate upwards if you're called in for an interview. You won't be rejected if you ask for $1,500 or $2,000 more than was mentioned in the job announcement or ad.

5. Keep the cover letter informal and conversational. The best business writing is conversational. Never use a phrase such as "enclosed please find," "under separate cover," or "thanking you in advance."

6. Don't use a form letter unless responding to a job advertised by an employment agency. If you have a portfolio of samples, say so, but avoid sending samples and never send your portfolio. By holding back your portfolio, you are sure of something to talk about when you eventually do get an interview.

7. Reorganize your portfolio for each interview according to the nature of each potential employer. If a place is looking for someone who primarily writes press releases, put all your press releases up front.

Now, a word about references:

- Avoid putting the names of references on your resume or cover letter. Supply them when you are close to getting the job. That way, your references won't be bothered by personnel people who are checking references just to fill up their time.

- Alert your references as to when they may be getting a call. Tell them about the job you've applied for so that they will be prepared to discuss your experience in light of the job you are seeking.

- Also: Collect and keep samples of every promotional piece you write, design, or edit. Keep all materials relating to elaborate direct-mail campaigns or press parties. It's more impressive to show an employer a direct-mail package when it is accompanied by a budget, a media list, and other bits of documentation that show you truly carried the project through to completion.

Your First Big Break

Your first break in public relations may be your first job or it may be your first client. It will give you the opportunity to discover whether or not you are cut out for the field.

In all probability, your first job will involve what engineers commonly refer to as "grunt work": answering letters, answering telephones, writing copy for mundane products or services, or simply compiling media lists. You may find yourself in press or consumer relations, political campaigning, fund-raising, or employee recruitment. Whatever you're doing, take good mental notes.

If you are at a small public relations agency, your break may come when you land your first substantial client. Suddenly, instead of writing the occasional release or fiddling with mailing lists, you'll be involved with such things as arranging press parties, placing feature articles, designing a direct-mail campaign, and working with designers and illustrators in creating brochures, logos, letterheads, and envelopes. This is your chance to fly. You'll see how much responsibility you can handle and how well you can do a number of tasks.

A neighborhood gourmet store gave one small, two-person agency the opportunity to get actively involved with the New York City food press. Their job was to launch a new $1 million gourmet store on the Upper East Side. The assignment called for a wide range of skills, and the two young men did everything from naming the store to organizing the opening-day press party. They both gained twenty pounds as they sampled the food so that they could write about it with conviction!

They wrote a three-page press release and a fact sheet describing some of the food that would be featured. Later on, they designed and implemented a direct-mail program that offered the store's catering services to food managers at New York's top corporations.

The account gave these young PR men a variety of clips and other samples of their work that they were able to parlay into gaining more food accounts. They could point to the stories they had placed in the *New York Times*, the *Daily News*, and the *Post*. They even managed to get the *Wall Street Journal* to mention the store on page one. Because the store owner gave full rein to the public relations specialists, they were able to create a logo, cover letters, brochures, and flyers that were well produced in addition to being well written. Most importantly, they gained rapport with the cream of the New York food press, which became a salable commodity when they pitched their services to other food accounts.

Clients require you to stretch yourself as a writer. The challenge is to make a press release so interesting and inviting that an editor will use it as the basis of a story. When you've placed a story, you've made everyone happy: yourself, the editor, and your client. You've also gained a "clip"—a press clipping—that you can use to demonstrate to other clients or employers that you have a track record.

Similarly, when you write your first brochure, you've gained a showcase for the quality of your writing. People will instinctively react to your work with the thought: If they've done this well in the past, they'll be able to help me in the future. So, your clips—brochures, media placements, flyers, and pamphlets—are your best selling tools. Public relations professionals are intensely interested in knowing who is responsible for a successful campaign. Although you may never get to sign your name to your feature stories or brochures, your reputation as a good publicist will spread.

To make yourself special, always take a special view of every task you perform. A simple press release can be transformed into something very unusual if you care enough to make your work first-rate. One young publicist, eager to find a hook for a release being written about an acupuncturist, did some investigative work and discovered that it had been ten years since Nixon's trip to China. He used the anniversary as the inspiration for the release's headline, "Ten Years After Nixon's Visit to China, Acupuncture Comes of Age." The release, which went on to focus on the work of a single New York acupuncturist, was widely picked up.

What to Shoot For

There is no single goal for people entering public relations because the field is so diverse. Some people want to start their own public relations company. They want the autonomy and the potential for profit that come with running their own business. They also enjoy the diverse activities that await them as head of their own agency, such as bringing in new clients, designing public relations programs, writing, creating graphics, and setting the fees for their services.

Other people want to climb the corporate communications ladder. Usually, that means becoming the communications director of a company, an association, or a government agency. The directorship may bring a high salary, an expense account, and other "perks," but it can require distancing yourself from the communication skills that brought you pleasure as you were coming up through the ranks.

When you get to be the boss, you may spend many afternoons taking care of administrative details, attending meetings, manipulating budgets, and writing memos, while your helpers write the releases, run the junkets, place the stories, and attend the photo sessions and press parties. While they're doing that, you may be planning policy and setting goals for others to reach.

Your goal should be the development of your own skills through increasing the diversity and depth of your experience in both print and broadcast media, making new contacts and maintaining old ones, and keeping abreast of new technologies and methods of printing, mailing, and placing promotions. Some of the larger public relations firms recognize the value of diverse experience and make mobility a part of their training programs.

Some people aim at becoming the head of a large public relations department or agency, whereas others prefer the challenge of a small department. In general, the larger the agency, the more it is specialized. You may spend several years doing work that is reported on time-sheets so that the clients can be billed accordingly. For those who rebel against the notion of time-sheets, there are less regimented, more congenial shops. And, of course, there is always the option of opening your own business. A number of new public relations firms start up when a person who has been working closely on one account woos that account into becoming the first client of his or her newly formed public relations firm.

When You've Made It

You've made it when you're doing what you want to be doing and are being paid well for it. If you're a writer, you may be content to go from high-priced project to high-priced project. Writers can make the move to account executive, aiming to move up the corporate ladder, but most creative people don't believe that more is necessarily better.

Some public relations people, however, relish the idea of implementing increasingly larger promotional projects. For instance, Herb Schmertz, director of corporate communications at Mobil Oil, has played a leading role in creating Mobil's image as a civic-minded corporation. Perhaps his boldest public-relations gambit was actually an advertising coup. By placing low-key, issues-oriented advertisements on the op-ed page of the *New York Times*, Schmertz persuaded the public to see Mobil as being concerned about the fight against industrial pollution, the high price of oil, and the search for alternative energy sources.

In the world of film and television public relations, John Springer of John Springer Associates has handled key moments in the careers of many top entertainers. He has been a quiet, effective buffer between clients and the press on numerous occasions, including some involving Elizabeth Taylor and Richard Burton. In a recent issue of *East Side TV Shopper*, a Manhattan magazine, Springer was asked why high-powered celebrities love him:

"They trust me. Twenty years ago I started this business, and set firm rules. Always work with people you admire. Never deal in scandal, or betray a client's confidence. I've been offered huge amounts of money to write a tell-all book but even after a client is long dead, it's contemptible to violate a special bond.

"I know the publicist stereotype. He is supposed to be this seedy stogie-smoking man who races to the nearest pay phone, dials a scandal sheet and purrs: 'Have I got a scoop for you.' But to survive, the publicist must be responsible and respectable."

Today, John Springer Associates publicizes numerous films, plays, books, the RKO Nederlander theaters, and Strawberry Shortcake, a popular character created by the American Greeting Corporation.

The firm of Rogers & Cowan has handled personal publicity, as well as corporate publicity, for many notables. Henry Rogers personally handled public relations during Prince Philip's extensive visit to the United States.

There have always been "kingmakers," people who stand behind political candidates and handle interpersonal, as well as public relations, functions. David Garth has achieved recognition for designing some of the cleverest public relations strategies for successful political candidates. For example, it was Garth who positioned Mayor John Lindsay in his successful bid for reelection with a campaign built around the candid admission, "I've made some mistakes."

I'll conclude this chapter by quoting from the Public Relations Society of America's booklet, titled "Careers in Public Relations":

"Basic to all public relations...is communicating. Well thought-out, effectively handled communications are increasingly seen as essential to the success and even existence of organizations and causes in today's complex, fast-changing world. Every organization—governmental, business, labor, professional and membership, health, cultural, educational, and public service—depends on people. Their attitudes, attention, understanding and motivation can be critical factors in whether an organization or an idea succeeds or fails."

Selected Reference Books in Public Relations

1982 All-In-One PR Directory. Gebbie Press, P.O. Box 1000, New Paltz, NY 12561. Lists more than 22,000 public relations outlets in nine different fields: daily newspapers, weekly newspapers, farm publications, television stations, AM-FM radio stations, consumer magazines, business and financial papers, trade publications, and outlets in the black press and radio.

Bacon's Publicity Checker (two volumes). Annual. Bacon Publishing Co., 14 E. Jackson Blvd., Chicago, IL 60604. Includes supplements; volumes not sold separately. The periodical volume is classified by subject or industry, with an alphabetical listing as well. The newspaper volume is in two parts—dailies and weeklies—with a geographical index. Both give detailed information about each publication (i.e., its location, circulation, issue dates, kinds of release sused, and executive staff members).

Becker, William B. *The TV News Handbook.* Insider's Guides, P.O. Box 2424, Southfield, MI 48037. Tells who to contact, what they're looking for, and how to slant stories to the decision makers.

Burrelle Annuals. Burrelle Co., 75 E. Northfield, Livingston, NJ 07039. Excellent local references. Volumes include: New York State, New Jersey, Pennsylvania, Connecticut, Maryland-Delaware, New England, Greater Boston, Special Groups (Minority, Ethnic).

Cable TV Publicity Outlets Nationwide. P.O. Box 327, Washington Depot, CT 06794. Lists over 660 contacts. Includes two completely updated and reprinted editions, printed semiannually.

The Encyclopedia of Associations (three volumes). Gale Research Company, Book Tower, Detroit, MI 48226. A comprehensive and definitive listing of 13,300 trade associations, professional societies, labor unions, fraternal and patriotic organizations, and other voluntary member groups. Entries include association, location, membership, size, objectives, activities, and publications.

O'Dwyer's Directory of Corporate Communications. Annual. A guide to twenty-four hundred companies and three hundred trade associations that are public-relations intensive. Entries include company name, address, telephone, sales and business activities, as well as names and duties of principal public relations personnel. Also gives names and addresses of outside public relations counsel, if any.

O'Dwyer's Directory of Public Relations Firms. 1983 Edition. J.R. O'Dwyer and Co., Inc., 271 Madison Ave., New York, NY 10010. Lists more than twelve hundred individual firms. Gives addresses, phone numbers, principles, numbers of employees, and areas of specialization.

Public Relations Handbook. Richard W. Darrow et. al., Dartnell, 4660 Ravenswood Ave., Chicago, IL 60640. Informative.

Radio Contacts. Larami Communications. A yearly directory on radio programming with twenty-five hundred major market station listings. Includes affiliates, personnel, format, local programs, guest, and information requirements. Network and syndicate listings include information on programs, contacts, and guest placements. Monthly "change bulletins" update information.

Television Contacts. Larami Communication Association, Ltd., 151 E. 50th St., New York, NY 10022. A yearly directory on national, syndicated, and local program guest, product, and informational requirements. Local listings include affiliation, personnel, addresses, and programs. Monthly "change bulletin" updates programs, personnel, and editorial requirements. Daily updating service available for major markets.

TV Publicity Outlets–Nationwide. P.O. Box 327, Washington Depot, CT 06794. Covers twenty-five hundred television program contacts. Includes three completely updated and reprinted editions, one every four months.

Weiver, Richard. *Syndicated Columnists.* Public Relations Publishing Company, 888 Seventh Ave., New York, NY 10006. Organizes columnists by subject matter.

Selected Public Relations Periodicals

Bulldog. California Business News, 6420 Wilshire Blvd., Suite 711, Los Angeles, CA 90048.

Communication Illustrated. P.O. Box 924, Bartlesville, OK 74005. Monthly.

Communicator's Journal: The Magazine of Applied Communications. P.O. Box 602, Downtown Station, Omaha, NE 68101.

Jack O'Dwyer's Newsletter. 271 Madison Ave., New York, NY 10016.

PR Aids Party Line. 221 Park Ave. S., New York, NY 10003. Weekly.

PR Calendar. 245 E. 40th St., Apt. 6E, New York, NY 10016. Weekly.

Public Relations Journal. Public Relations Society of America, 845 Third Ave., New York, NY 10017. Monthly.

Public Relations News. 127 E. 80th St., New York, NY 10021. Weekly.

Public Relations Review. Communication Research Associates, Inc., Suite 500, 7100 Baltimore Blvd., College Park, MD 20740. Quarterly.

Publicist. 221 Park Ave. S., New York, NY 10003. Bimonthly.

Social Science Monitor For Public Relations and Advertising Executives. Communication Research Associates, Inc., Suite 500, 7100 Baltimore Blvd., College Park, MD 20740. Monthly.

Speechwriter's Newsletter. 407 S. Dearborn, Chicago, IL 60605. Weekly.

Three Major Public Relations Organizations

The Professional Development Institute for Public Relations/Communications Professionalism. Pace University, 331 Madison Ave., Room 603, New York, NY 10017. Offers training resources in a wide variety of public relations areas.

Public Affairs Council (PAC). 1220 16th St., NW, Washington, DC 20036. Its members are corporate public affairs executives who want to encourage the business community to be active in public affairs. The Council provides public-affairs training seminars, workshops, and counseling for corporations beginning public affairs programs. Meets semiannually. Founded: 1954. Publications: Materials on public affairs, *Directory of Public Affairs Officers*, annual.

Public Relations Society of America (PRSA). 845 Third Ave., New York, NY 10022. A professional society for people in public relations in business, industry, government, trade and professional groups, and nonprofit organizations. Offers continuing education programs and an executive referral service. Founded: 1948. Publications: *Channels*, monthly; *Public Relations Journal*, monthly; *Public Relations Register*, annual.

The 15 Largest Public Relations Agencies in the United States

1. Hill and Knowlton
   420 Lexington Ave.
   New York, NY 10017
   Offices around the world.

2. Burson-Marsteller
   866 Third Ave.
   New York, NY 10022

3. Carl Byoir & Associates
   380 Madison Ave.
   New York, NY 10017
   Offices around the world.

4. Ruder Finn & Rotman
   110 E. 59th St.
   New York, NY 10022
   Offices around the world

5. Daniel J. Edelman
   221 N. LaSalle St.
   Chicago, IL 60601
   Offices in New York, Washington, D.C., Los Angeles,
   London, and Frankfurt.

6. The Rowland Company
   415 Madison Ave.
   New York, NY 10017

7. Manning, Selvage & Lee
   99 Park Ave.
   New York NY 10017

8. Ketchum Communications
   4 Gateway Center
   Pittsburgh, PA 15222

9. Doremus & Company
   120 Broadway
   New York, NY 10271

10. Rogers & Cowan
    9665 Wilshire Blvd.
    Beverly Hills, CA 90212

11. Ogilvy & Mather Public Relations
    964 Third Ave.
    New York, NY 10022

12. Booke Communications Incorporated Group
    355 Lexington Ave.
    New York, NY 10022

13. Creamer Dickson Basford
    1633 Broadway
    New York, NY 10022

14. Bozell & Jacobs Public Relations
    1 Dag Hammerskjold Plaza
    New York, NY 10022

15. Robert Marston & Associates
    485 Madison Ave.
    New York, NY 10022

Public Relations: A Few Terms of the Trade

Backgrounder. Information supplied to the press that gives the background of a product, service, person, or organization.

Comp. This term is used in two different ways—as short for "complimentary," or free, as when applied to tickets for public events such as films, plays, or concerts; or as short for "comprehensive," which is a rough layout of a printed piece that allows for further input before more detailed work is begun.

Contact. The person identified in promotional material as being a source of further information.

Demographics. Specific information about groups of people—age, sex, location, education, income level—that may form a market for your product or service.

Designer/Art Director. A person involved in giving direction and shape to graphics. Includes the choosing of artistic elements involved in a promotion (e.g., logo, type size and style, paper, ink).

Dog and Pony Show. A public relations and advertising term referring to an elaborate presentation made to impress a potential client. Originally a circus expression, the phrase connotes a presentation filled with impressive visuals, one that pulls out all the stops.

Fact Sheet. The part of a press kit that lists key facts, such as who founded the company, when it was founded, or the number of employees. It is used to supplement a press release and other elements of a press kit.

Flack. A derogatory reference to a publicist.

Pitch Letter. A letter asking for a particular response. It can be used to "pitch" a product or service by asking the recipient to place features, arrange interviews, or participate in a press conference or special event.

Point-of-Purchase Display. A method of displaying a product at the location where it is sold.

Portfolio. A notebook or carrying case filled with samples of your work, such as articles for the school paper, sample press releases, sample designs, or anything else relevant to your work in public relations. It is also known as a "book."

Sales Promotion. Any endeavor that is meant to increase sales or awareness of a particular product or service, but is neither advertising (paid space) nor public relations (editorial influence). Included in sales promotion are sales contests for retailers or distributors, brochures, and flyers.

Tip Sheet. A press release aimed at the broadcast media, showing how a
  client offers valuable tips to a listening or viewing audience. A book
  publisher might send a tip sheet about a new book to a program
  director or producer, to encourage him or her to schedule the author as
  a guest on the talk show.

Two-, Three-, Four-, or Five-Color. The number of different colors applied
  to a printed piece.

CHAPTER   SEVEN

The Corporate World

*I*t's ironic: Many people become writers to escape the perceived drudgery of the nine-to-five corporate life. Yet corporations are a prime source of employment for writers, and a large number of writers are not aware of the many opportunities in this market.

Pros and Cons

Cons First

There is a downside to being a corporate writer. To begin with, you lose all the perks that come with being an independent writer. You have a nine-to-five job. You have to commute and wear business clothes. You have a boss who tells you what to do. You must deal with office politics and work in an environment that, to you, may be less than ideal. You are expected to come in, be at your desk, take lunch, and leave at hours your employer sets. If you have to work long hours, in most cases you won't get paid extra. You spend a lot of your time in meetings and dealing with other people.

Another problem: With the recent downsizing in corporate America today, there are still staff jobs for writers, but there are far fewer of them. So competition for jobs is stiff. When I joined Westinghouse as a staff writer in 1979, it was relatively easy to get a corporate writing job. Now it is more difficult.

Also, surveys indicate that corporate workers are working longer hours now than in years past. And corporate writers are no exception. Although salaries have not risen dramatically, hours are more demanding, and writers, as professionals, are not compensated for the overtime.

What's the reason for the extended hours? Downsizing once again is the culprit. Companies have never had large writing staffs compared with other departments such as accounting or engineering. For instance, the Westinghouse location at which I was a staff writer had approximately eight thousand employees. The total number of staff writers was less than three dozen.

And even those numbers are shrinking. Today I see corporations letting their technical publications departments go, keeping only a manager on staff, and outsourcing the work to free-lancers or contract firms. Communications departments that once had a dozen employees are now down to one or two. Much of the writing is farmed out to free-lancers and ad agencies, or even done in-house by engineers, managers, and other nonwriters. All of this means that there are fewer positions available today than when I got my first corporate job in 1979.

Another drawback: Corporate writers often are not highly respected, either by their coworkers or fellow writers. Many managers think writing is relatively unimportant and can be done by anybody. Engineers look down upon it as a minor skill. Writers are somewhat out of the mainstream of the company's core business, so they often are not seen as critical to the team.

Literary-type writers look down on corporate writing as boring and mundane. Journalists often think of corporate writers as hacks who have sold out, writing hype rather than the truth. Magazine and book authors view corporate writers as "unpublished," even though these writers have produced numerous booklets, videos, manuals, and pamphlets for their employers.

Now the Pros

Being a corporate writer has its upside, too. First, you don't have to sell and market your services. The aspect of writing as a career most independent writers enjoy least is selling—pursuing business, attending meetings, making presentations, setting prices, negotiating fees and deadlines, billing, and making collections.

Staff writers are freed of these unpleasant tasks. Each day, you come into work and a boss gives you work to do. You are paid the same every week regardless of the work load or the assignments. You don't renegotiate your fee every week; you just get a salary increase about once a year.

There are other advantages as well. You are given a computer, a place to work, office supplies, medical insurance, sick days, personal days, vacation days, a salary, a telephone, and a fax machine. Independent writers must supply these for themselves. In addition, you get a steady paycheck, week after week. Independents have irregular cash flow, dependent on how good the marketing part of your work has been. Corporate life provides the structure and routine many people desire or need.

Corporate life offers one other important benefit: a social environment. Writing is a lonely occupation. Most writers sit alone in a room all day in front of a computer and type. Corporate writers have much more contact with people during the day than the average free-lance writer. Many people enjoy the social atmosphere of the office—the joking, the camaraderie, the friendships.

What Positions Are Available?

You should be aware of the fact that most corporate jobs advertised as "writing" jobs may not entail much actual writing. While some writing jobs are "pure" writing jobs, in that your main function is to write, other writing jobs are really print production jobs. Not only do you write technical and promotional material, but you are responsible for its publication. That means you spend more time working with graphic designers, dealing with printers, supervising photographers and illustrators, reading galleys, and getting manuscripts approved than you do writing. For writers who would rather write than get involved in the detailed work of print production, this is a drawback. For people who like to write but get bored doing nothing but writing, it's a plus.

Check the help-wanted ads in newspapers and industry trade journals. You will find corporations advertising the following positions, all of which are writing or writing-related jobs:

- Technical publications manager

- Technical writer

- Technical editor

- Proofreader

- Production manager

- Copy editor

- Proposal writer

- Employee communications manager

- Marketing communications manager

- Advertising manager

- Writer

- Copywriter

- Marketing manager

- Investor relations manager

- Corporate communications manager

- Manager of public relations

- Director of public affairs

- Communications director

- Newsletter editor

- Specifications writer

- Manual writer

- Promotions manager

I would classify these jobs into three categories: jobs that are mostly writing; jobs that are mostly print production and project management; and jobs that are strategic or managerial or involve planning and strategy. The above list doesn't divide neatly into these three categories because the jobs listed fall into different categories at different companies, depending on the employer's philosophy and the job description.

Let's discuss what writers do in corporations and who they do it for.

Writing Jobs

Although there are fewer positions that I would consider strictly writing jobs today, such jobs do exist.

No writer spends one hundred percent of his or her time writing. There are many other tasks one must attend to. In a corporation, a "writing job" is any job in which 20 to 50 percent of the employee's hours are spent writing or doing writing-related tasks (interviewing, editing, researching).

The greatest demand for writers in corporate America is for technical writers to produce manuals, proposals, reports, and other business and technical documents. Writers are also needed to do annual reports, employee newsletters, articles for company magazines, and press releases. Many corporations have staff writers who primarily write speeches for executives.

Corporate writers do not primarily write what they want. Their job is to interpret the thoughts of others—managers, product specialists, salespeople, executives—and translate them into clear, interesting, persuasive booklets, reports, speeches, press releases, and advertisements. The creativity is often not in originating the project or theme, but in writing a translation that is readable and lively yet survives the bureaucratic approval process and conforms to acceptable company policy.

There are no statistics on salary for corporate writers. My research shows that a salary of $40,000 to $60,000 a year is typical. Beginners and strictly technical writers may earn less, and speech writers working for top executives can pass the $90,000-a-year mark in some corporations. The pay for corporate writers is better than what most other writers earn and equal to or slightly less than what others in staff and middle management positions in the corporate world make.

Project Management

I know many people who have positions classified as "writing" but in fact do little or no writing. They start off as writers, but their jobs are more involved with project management. They spend their days doing the various tasks necessary to get printed materials published. These include:

- getting printing quotes

- hiring photographers and illustrators

- working with graphic artists

- getting copy and layouts approved

- supervising production and printing

- inserting advertisements in magazines

- reserving booth space at trade shows

- mailing press releases to magazines and newspapers

- planning and organizing meetings, press conferences, seminars, and other events

- maintaining photo and slide visuals

- purchasing advertising specialty items

- creating production budgets and schedules

- acting as liaison with the company's advertising agency

- getting trade show displays built and shipped

- attending meetings

The job title may be specific to project management—production manager, manager of technical publications, advertising administrator, communications coordinator—or it may sound like a writing job—technical writer, marketing communications representative, promotions copywriter—but actually entail mostly project management and very little writing.

More and more corporate writing jobs fall into this project management category and involve even more project management than they used to. Most corporations today have smaller communications staffs. When the staff is smaller, those remaining becoming managers and coordinators rather than writers. Writing is done by ad agency personnel, free-lancers, or other employees for whom writing is not a primary duty. The staff communications people edit the writing, get it approved, and put it into production; but often they do not write original drafts.

Corporate Management

Sometimes writers, who can also be thinkers and strategists, go beyond writing and project management to become part of the management team. Usually writers are managers in one of these areas: sales, marketing, product management, public relations, corporate communications, employee communications, human resources, training and development, or community relations.

As a manager, your role may consist of a little writing and editing, some project management, employee supervision, planning, and strategy. You will work with ideas, expressing them in memos, reports, plans, and letters; but you will not be a "writer" as such. Many writers who grow tired of the routine of writing or managing print production jump at the chance to grab a managerial position. The responsibility is greater, and your annual salary will be at least $10,000 or so higher.

As a writer, you may feel you lack project management or leadership skills. These can be learned. However, it's best to do what you enjoy, so if it's writing you want, be aware that many corporate writing positions actually involve doing other types of work.

There is nothing wrong with asking a potential employer, "How much writing is actually involved with this job?" If less than one hour a day will be spent writing, it is a management or project management position. If you will actually spend one to two hours a day or more writing, I would consider it a writing job. Remember, not all of a writer's day is spent writing; there are many other tasks. Even free-lancers spend only 50 to 60 percent of their time writing and the rest at other activities. Don't expect to spend 100 percent of your time writing. It isn't realistic.

Where to Look

Corporate staff writing jobs are almost never advertised in the writer's magazines. The best place to find openings is by checking the help-wanted ads in your local Sunday newspaper. Look under such categories as "advertising," "public relations," "marketing," "corporate communications," and "technical writing."

Career counselors and job seekers debate whether it is better to respond to help-wanted ads, go through executive recruiters, network, or write directly to employers. Each has its pros and cons. A combination of the three usually works best.

The advantage of replying to an ad is that you know the company has a current job opening. The disadvantage is that this opening is advertised; therefore, you will be competing with dozens or hundreds of other applicants. To give you an idea of the response help-wanted ads can generate, I once placed a tiny classified ad with the title "Technical Writers Wanted" in the Sunday *New York Times*. The ad, which cost ninety-five dollars, was smaller than one inch, and ran once, generated nearly one hundred resumes. So competition for jobs, even when the employer is not named or not well known, is fierce.

Join local business groups such as chambers of commerce and advertising clubs. Often their newsletters advertise writing jobs that you might not see in the regular newspaper.

If you have friends or acquaintances working at corporations, ask them if they can get postings of new job listings for you. Some writing positions are posted internally before they are advertised in the newspaper. If you get word of them early, you have a leg up on your competition.

How to Apply

Apply to appealing positions with a standard resume and cover letter. A couple of pointers specifically for job-seeking writers:

First, since it's a writing job, your resume and cover letter must be flawless. Typos or even clumsily worded applications will eliminate you as a potential candidate. Interestingly, one recruiter reported that two-thirds of all resumes she saw contained at least one typo. This won't ruin your chance of being hired if you are an engineer or chemist, but it's a deadly mistake for a writer.

Second, a brilliantly written resume and cover letter, while helpful, won't clinch the job for you. What will? Experience or knowledge of the company's industry is a plus that can separate you from other candidates. So is experience writing the particular types of documents the company needs to produce. For instance, if you are applying to be a speech writer for International Paper, you should mention if you have written speeches previously or worked in the paper or printing industries.

Should you enclose samples of your writing with your cover letter and resume? Probably not. The danger is that the sample is not exactly what they are looking for, and will turn them off. However, if you have a sample that is brilliant, relevant to their needs, and would be of interest, send it. Just send one or two, though. In your cover letter, mention your other samples or portfolio, if such is available.

Cold-Call Mailing

In addition to responding to help-wanted ads, you can send letters and resumes to companies in your area. These can be companies in your geographic region or in the industry or field where you want to work. The resources at the end of this chapter tell where to get names and addresses of potential employers for a letter-writing campaign.

Tell the prospective employer your qualifications, the type of job you want, and then ask for an interview if there are current openings or will be in the near future. Write to the manager in charge of the department for which you would work (marketing, human resources, communications, technical publications), not the personnel or human resources manager. Be sure to write to the individual by name. A quick telephone call to the switchboard operator or receptionist can generally provide the information you need.

Some career advisors suggest writing and requesting "informational interviews"—telling people you just want to talk with them about opportunities in their industry or their company and are not immediately looking for a job. To me this is too indirect. If you want a job, say so. If you get turned down and still think it would be beneficial to speak with that person for information-gathering purposes, call and request an appointment. Many will be glad to talk with you.

Networking

While job hunting, it does pay to make yourself visible and get your name around. Attend industry meetings, especially local chapter meetings of trade and professional societies to which potential employers belong. Let people know you are looking for a job and have resumes or business cards with your name and phone number available.

Usually you won't meet an employer directly. Instead, someone in the group will refer you to someone who knows someone. That second, third, or fourth person down the chain is hiring and will interview you based largely on the fact that you were referred by someone known and trusted. Take advantage of this networking opportunity whenever it is available.

Recently I spoke at a direct-marketing industry event. A client who attended confided that he was looking for a new job and asked me to refer him if I heard of any openings. I knew he liked his job and expressed surprise that he was considering a move. "Don't kid yourself," he said. "Ninety percent of the people here are looking either for a job or clients. They don't come for the workshops or the education." An important lesson to keep in mind!

Headhunters

Corporate writing jobs generally pay between $25,000 and $85,000 a year, although some pay more. At these salary levels, executive search firms can make a profit recruiting writers, just as they make money recruiting engineers, technicians, and middle managers.

The thing to remember is that the executive search firms work for the employers, not the job seekers. They are paid by the employer when they find an acceptable person for the position; they are not paid by job seekers when they get the job seeker a position.

Many job seekers rely too heavily on executive search firms to find them employment. You should view contacting headhunters as an ancillary activity. It may indeed result in interviews and a job offer. But don't count on it. If you want to get a corporate writing job, it will probably come through your own efforts. Concentrate on mailings, replying to help-wanted ads, and networking. These avenues are more likely to yield an offer than executive search firms, although they are definitely worth including in your mix of job hunting activities, since you never know from where an offer may come.

It is a mistake to count on a headhunter to take a personal interest in you or your quest for a job. They may act interested in you, but that interest occurs only if they have a position which they think they can fill with you. Executive recruiters get paid for results, not effort. Therefore, the longer it takes to fill a position, and the more candidates they advertise for and interview, the lower their profit on the assignment.

If a recruiter thinks his client would be interested in hiring you, he'll be enthusiastic. But if the client does not want to hire you, and there are no immediate positions with other clients that you can fill, the recruiter will quickly lose interest in you. It's on to the next resume, the next candidate, the next interview. They are not in business to be your friend or career counselor, or help solve your unemployment or career-change problem. They are in business to make money. If you can help them do that, fine. If not, spending more time with you will not be productive for them.

Getting Around in Corporate America

You may not have previously worked in corporate America, let alone worked as a writer in a corporation. What is it like?

New Yorker cartoons portray corporate America as conformist, stuffy, traditional, and dull. There is some truth to this, but the dullness is greatly exaggerated. My experience is that writers who opt for corporate employment are realists. Idealists become reporters and journalists or write socially important books. Artistic and literary writers pursue the writing of novels, short stories, poems, plays, and essays.

Some writers have these dreams only when they are young. Others pursue them for decades; some even throughout their lives. Some achieve varying degrees of success in literary pursuits; others don't.

Writers choose the corporate route for several reasons. One is the regularity of work and a paycheck. The benefits offered by large corporations are also an attraction.

Is corporate work inherently boring? I don't believe so. Corporate writing, while not perhaps what you dreamed of when in high school or college, can be extremely rewarding, creative, fun, and challenging. Personally, I enjoy it very much. Part of whether you enjoy this work depends on the attitude you bring to it. If you can view the constraints of writing for a corporate purpose as a creative challenge, you'll find the work stimulating. If you have a negative image of corporate America, and feel you are compromising your dreams to do this work, you will be less happy.

What about ethics? Does accepting a job with a corporation mean that you, as a writer and human being, are selling out? Again, I do not believe so. If you've worked in corporations, you know that the majority of companies—and the majority of people they employ—are not evil or malicious. Most want to earn a profit or a salary by providing goods and services that people need and want to buy. What's wrong with helping to promote good products to people who can benefit from them?

I have spoken with some journalists who view what they do as a higher calling and what corporate, advertising, and public relations writers do as hack work. Is this an accurate perception? There may be some shades of truth to it, but I think it is a misinterpretation of reality. The challenges in writing to persuade and inform can be met with creativity and integrity in both corporate and journalistic assignments.

What is Different Today?

Although I have not worked as a staff writer for a corporation since 1982, I have many clients and colleagues who hold such positions. Based on discussions and observation, corporate life is more difficult today than when I was a staff writer more than a decade ago.

Because of downsizing, there are fewer staff writers, editors, and managers in most organizations. Yet the work load has not diminished. If anything, it has increased. Deadlines are tighter, supervisors more demanding. Therefore, corporate writers are working longer and harder.

When I was a staff writer, we came in at eight or nine in the morning and rarely worked past 5 P.M. or on weekends. Now, many corporate communications professionals put in long hours, take work home, and go in on weekends. Yet they are not paid overtime or given larger salaries. I feel writers and others in corporations today are definitely working harder to earn a living.

With the increased hours and work load come more pressure and stress. My two corporate staff writing positions were relatively easy and stress free. Today corporate writers, just like free-lancers, are constantly up against deadlines and rushing to get a lot of work done for many people on schedule and within budget.

To be fair, it's not just the writers who are so pressured and harried. Virtually everyone I know in corporate America today is working more hours, has too much to do, and not enough time to do it.

Corporate life, once modestly paced for most employees except senior executives and upper management, has become stressful and pressured. In the past, writers who wanted out of the high-stress ad agency career switched to being advertising managers in corporations. Now both positions involve plenty of overtime and hard work.

Corporate America has downsized and restructured, and I think this change is permanent. Corporate jobs, while lucrative, are not easy and probably never will be again. If you want the money and security of a corporate position, be prepared for the hard work and long hours that go with it.

The Bottom Line

Is corporate life for you? On the plus side, it offers a regular salary, benefits, a social structure, a comfortable environment, regularity, security, and fairly decent compensation. Most corporate writers earn considerably more than their counterparts who write for newspapers. On the negative side, corporate life lacks the excitement and freedom of free-lancing, the artistic fulfillment of fiction, and the prestige of being a "real" author with published articles and books.

Personally, I enjoyed my corporate positions when I had them. I became a free-lancer primarily because my employer wanted to relocate me, and I didn't want to go. Many free-lancers rave about how superior free-lancing is to full-time employment. In my mind, each has its pros and cons, although many corporate employees are convinced they would be happier self-employed. I'm not so certain.

My advice? Why not try both. The more writing positions you hold, the more diverse your experience and the fuller your portfolio. Your marketability and versatility increase. You get to experience many writing careers and then choose the one most satisfying to you. Sounds like a no-lose proposition to me.

Resources

The Encyclopedia of Associations (three volumes). Gale Research Company, Book Tower, Detroit, Ml 48226. A comprehensive and definitive listing of 13,300 trade associations, professional societies, labor unions, fraternal and patriotic organizations, and other voluntary member groups. Entries include association name, location, membership, size, objectives, activities, and publications.

O'Dwyer's Directory of Corporation Communications. J.R. O'Dwyer and Co., Inc., 271 Madison Ave., New York, NY 10010. An annual guide to 2,400 companies and 300 trade associations that are public-relations intensive. Entries include company name, address, telephone, sales and business activities, as well as names and duties of principal public relations personnel. Also gives names and addresses of outside public relations counsel, if any.

The Standard Directory of Advertisers. National Register Publishing Company, 3004 Glenview Rd., Wilmette, IL 60091. Lists 17,000 companies that spend $30,000 a year or more on advertising. Each listing includes the company name and address, key personnel, products manufactured, and the size of the ad budget.

Technical Writing

Newspaper reporters and technical writers are trained to reveal almost nothing about themselves in their writing. This makes them freaks in the world of writers, since almost all of the other ink-stained wretches in that world reveal a lot about themselves to the readers. —KURT VONNEGUT, JR., NOVELIST AND FORMER TECHNICAL PUBLICIST FOR GENERAL ELECTRIC

Most technical writers would hardly classify themselves as "freaks in the world of writers." Yet technical writing, the literature of science and technology, is different from journalism, fiction, advertising copywriting, and other nontechnical prose.

Just what is technical writing? To begin, technical writing is defined by its subject matter—it is writing that deals with subjects of a technical nature. By *technical* we mean anything that has to do with the specialized areas of science and industry.

Traditionally technical writers have been thought of as "engineering writers." However, in addition to engineering and applied sciences, technical writers are involved in all areas of physical, natural, and social sciences, including anthropology, archaeology, biology, botany, earth science, ecology, geology, management science, medicine, psychology, sociology, and zoology, to name a few.

Because technical writing usually deals with an object, a process, or an abstract idea, the language is utilitarian, stressing accuracy rather than style. The tone is objective; the technical content, not the author's voice, is the focal point.

The difference between technical writing and ordinary composition is more than just content, however. The two differ in purpose as well. The primary goal of any technical communication is to *accurately transmit technical information*. Thus it differs from popular nonfiction, in which the writing is intended to entertain, or from advertising copywriting, which exists to persuade. Technical writers are concerned with communication, and if they have to, they will sacrifice style, grace, and technique for clarity, precision, and organization.

Since the intended goal of any technical writing is the transmittal of technical information, even the most well-written technical document is ineffective if the facts, theories, and observations presented are in error. The content must be true and as scientifically accurate as possible. Technical writing that contains technically inaccurate statements reflects inadequate knowledge of the subject and poor use of language.

Why is technical accuracy more important in technical writing than in popular magazine articles, books, and other nonfiction? Technical documents are not merely leisure reading; their readers make business decisions and scientific judgments based on the data presented. An error in a Sunday supplement newspaper story may result in misinformed readers and nothing more. Errors in technical documents can cost industry hundreds of thousands of dollars, and the results of good scientific work can be obscured by hastily prepared reports that are full of inaccuracies.

How to Make a Living as a Technical Writer

If you have a strong interest in science and technology and like to write, technical writing might be the profession for you. Because many technical professionals write poorly, technical writers are needed in all areas of science and industry. These are some of the jobs that technical writers handle:

- Editing and proofreading copy

- Ghostwriting trade journal articles

- Working with engineers to help them improve their writing

- Producing a wide variety of technical publications, including letters, memorandums, manuals, proposals, papers, reports, abstracts, product literature, advertisements, press releases, scripts, charts, and tables

- Advising others in the organization about writing, graphics, printing, and binding methods

- Providing authors with writing, editing, and research assistance

- Preparing a writing style manual for the organization

- Helping technical people with their speeches and presentations

- Producing slide shows, films, and videotapes

You do not need a degree in science or engineering to write or edit technical publications. Although many full-time technical writers were scientists and engineers first, the majority came from the humanities, and the ranks are full of former English teachers, editors, journalists, and writers. The would-be technical writer has three basic employment options: full-time, contract, and free-lance work.

Full-time technical writers hold staff positions with scientific and technical organizations. A technical writer at a large company might work in a group solely devoted to producing manuals, proposals, or product literature. A technical editor at a trade journal works with contributing authors, preparing their manuscripts for publication. A small industrial manufacturer might hire one writer to handle all its technical communications.

The best place to find out about these jobs is the Sunday help wanted section of your largest local daily newspaper (look under Technical Writers, Writers, or Editors). As with any other professional position, you apply by sending a letter of application and a resume to your prospective employer. The one difference is that the resumes of many technical writers stress descriptions of the types of publications they have handled rather than a strict chronological listing of past employment by job title and company. A sample technical writing resume appears at the end of this chapter.

Contract work is an attractive alternative to full-time employment. It offers the regularity of nine-to-five business hours without chaining the writer to one job with one organization.

When an organization needs extra technical personnel, it can contract their services through a "temporary employment contractor." These employment contractors provide scientists, engineers, technicians, and technical writers on a temporary basis for days, weeks, months, and sometimes years. The temporary employees work at the organization's place of business but are paid by the employment contractor.

To get contract assignments, send several copies of your technical writing resume to the employment contractor. You can find these contractors listed in the Yellow Pages under Employment Contractors, Temporary; Temporary Help; Technical Writing Services; or Editorial Services. The contractor will keep your resume on file and will call you when an assignment comes in that matches your background and qualifications. Beginning technical writers can expect to earn between $10 and $25 per hour; an experienced writer can make $40 to $45 per hour. (You can earn even more if you have experience in an unusual or a highly specialized technical field that is in great demand.)

Free-lancing offers even more freedom than contract work. As a free-lancer, you won't be locked into the corporate structure and the Monday-through-Friday workweek. Free-lancers can sleep until noon if they want to.

Every year, a quarter of a million people in the United States go into business for themselves. If you want to join them, you need to do a few things first:

1. *Put some money in the bank.* It takes time for any new business to show a profit. Before you leave the security of your job for the uncertainties of free-lance life, you should have enough money saved up to live for at least six months without any income.

2. *Decide exactly what you want to do.* What services will you offer your clients—writing, editing, graphics and printing? Are you strictly technical, or will you take assignments in other areas? You must decide what your business is—preferably before you start it.

3. *Promote yourself.* Now that you are on your own, you must go out and *get clients.* Free-lancers, like industrial manufacturers, need sales literature—a brochure or resume that describes your business, the services you offer, your background and qualifications, and your fees. To get assignments, you could mail this brochure with a cover letter to organizations that could be potential clients. You might also promote yourself through publicity and advertising in technical magazines.

4. *Set your fees.* As a free-lance writer, you receive no bonuses, medical benefits, company insurance policies, sick days, or vacation. Therefore, your hourly rate must be higher than what you would get as a full-time employee. The going rate for free-lance technical writers ranges from $10 an hour for beginning technical editors to $75 an hour and up for experienced industrial advertising writers.

If you understand the basics of science and technology and can demonstrate an ability to write and think clearly, you should have no trouble making a good living as a technical writer, whether full-time, contract, or free-lance. Today the technical fields are booming, while the writing skills of college graduates are declining. Therefore, people who can write well on technical subjects are in demand. As a rule, technical writers earn slightly less than scientists and engineers, but more than writers and editors in non-technical fields.

Estimating a Technical Writing Job

One of the greatest difficulties in technical writing is determining how much to charge. If you are on staff, you have a salary, so what to charge for a data sheet, manual, or report isn't an issue: You're paid by the week, not by production.

Technical writers who work as contract writers perform the same work as staff writers but are not employees of the company. They are temporary workers paid by the hour or by the day. We have already discussed the rates. Because contract workers are compensated on a per-diem basis, they don't usually have to worry about estimating writing fees for any given task, and their pay is not tied directly to production—although a contract tech writer who does not produce his or her fair share of work will be let go faster than an underproducing staff writer.

Independent technical writers (free-lancers) and some quasi-contract technical writers are required by employers and clients to give some sort of estimate for the time and cost of writing a particular project. Estimates can be presented as a fixed project price, a per-page rate, or an estimated project fee based on estimated number of hours times the hourly rate.

Writing projects come together in three stages. First, research and study to learn the subject. Second, create an outline. Then, finally, settle into writing and re-writing. Each of these activities requires time and you must learn to estimate the amount of time needed. Here are some guidelines for preparing an estimate.

When estimating writing jobs, remember there are *always* delays. You can't charge for them, but the customer will not get around to approving the manuscript as promptly as you need it, you'll wait days for vital information, and you'll often find yourself sitting idle *on that project*. (The best answer is to have more than one project going. If you're also writing fiction, turn the time to finishing that story, novel, or screenplay. A writer can always use time productively.)

The first step in estimating a job is doing preliminary research and study. This involves gathering whatever information the client has available and discussing the project with the company's technical people in some detail. Gather enough material during your first interview to estimate the length of the project and the amount of time needed per page. This is done prior to making the sale or getting the assignment unless your client prefers paying you by the hour.

Never quote a job on the spot unless you have enough experience at estimating projects to be reasonably certain of your accuracy. Take the research materials home and study them until you are conversational on the subject. This shouldn't take more than a few hours, since you haven't done complete research.

Next, do a preliminary outline. It won't be accurate because you haven't enough detail, but don't worry about that. What you are trying to do is get a feel for how many pages will be involved in each major subject of the manual. After you've done a few projects, you'll find you can usually be accurate to within three to five pages. Remember to define the number of illustrations that will be required in each section, and allow for the space they'll take up in the page estimates.

Now consider the degree of difficulty. How much time will you need to absorb the subject, organize it, prepare a glossary, and write the manual? Figure between one and four hours per page as a base rate. If the subject is simple, but lengthy, an hour or two per page may do it. If it's a very technical subject, it may take you two to four hours per page.

The rule is: The longer the writing project, *the fewer hours per page you will average*. Short projects will come well up to the four-hour mark. Projects of one hundred pages or more will often come in at one-and-a-half hours or less, even when technically difficult.

Keep in mind that you will spend several days at the client company doing research and handling manuscript review meetings. Allow two to four full days for this on a hundred-page manuscript. Highly technical subjects may require more. In addition, you'll spend anywhere from one to three weeks doing nothing but study before you even submit an outline to the client.

Your final consideration is purely personal. What are your abilities? How long does it take you to learn and, once you've learned, how many pages per day can you produce? At a conservative estimate, you'll probably do two re-writes (I have done as many as six on a single project).

To accurately estimate time and cost for a project, do preliminary research and study, do a rough preliminary outline, and estimate the total number of pages needed, including text, illustrations, and glossary. Then estimate the number of hours per page you will average on that subject. Next, multiply your hourly rate ($25 to $50 per hour) by the estimated number of hours per page, and quote that as a firm per-page rate. Also quote the *estimated* number of pages in the job and the *estimated* total price (number of pages time the page rate). Be very sure you quote these last as estimates; your client should understand that he or she will pay the page rate, and the final fee will be based on the actual number of pages in the final draft.

For example, an *estimated* hundred-page manual at a firm rate of $100 per page would have an *estimated total price* of $10,000. But if the project totaled only ninety pages on the final draft, the client would pay $9,000.

There is a simple alternative, if you're nervous about missing the estimate. Persuade your client to pay you by the hour. You'll have to keep and submit accurate time records, but doing a few hourly rate projects allows you to gain experience before committing yourself to an estimate.

Be honest with your clients. If you've already got a project, explain that you'll start theirs during idle time on your current project, and put them next in line for completion (unless you've already promised that to someone else).

Most companies demand a performance schedule and expect you to keep it. Often there is a projected time table for each phase of the project. If you want repeat business from a company, promise only what you can deliver. Anything else weakens your chances of doing future work for that company—and will possibly destroy your reputation in your local market. Executives in these companies pass the word around about their bad experiences with suppliers. It takes long, hard work to build a good reputation. One false promise can tear all of that hard work down and put you in a worse position than when you started.

Where to Find More Information on Technical Writing

When you need more detailed information, you can consult the books and publications listed below. I especially recommend the *U.S. Government Printing Office Style Manual* for its complete coverage of numbers, grammar, punctuation, abbreviation, and capitalization, and the ASTM's *Standard for Metric Practice* for its thorough presentation of SI units.

Books and Documents

American Society for Testing and Materials (ASTM). *Standard for Metric Practice*, Philadelphia, document E-380-79, 1980.

Bernstein, Theodore M. *The Careful Writer: A Guide to English Usage.* New York: Atheneum, 1967.

Berry, Thomas Elliot. *The Most Common Mistakes in English Usage.* New York: McGraw-Hill, 1971.

Flesch, Rudolph. *The Art of Readable Writing.* New York: Harper & Row, 1949.

Follett, Wilson. *Modern American Usage.* New York: Hill & Wang, 1966.

Morrisey, George L. *Effective Business and Technical Presentations.* 2d ed., Reading, MA: Addison-Wesley, 1975.

Smith, Terry C. *How to Write Better and Faster.* New York: Thomas Y. Crowell, New York, 1965.

Strunk, William, Jr., and E. B. White. *The Elements of Style.* 3d ed. New York: Macmillan, 1979.

U.S. *Government Printing Office Style Manual.* Washington, DC: U.S. Government Printing Office (GPO), 1973.

Periodicals

The Journal of Technical Writing and Communications. Baywood Publishing Company, Inc., Box A-114, Wantagh, NY 11793.

Rogers' Tek Pubs Newsletter. 1735 Robinson, P.O. Box 2458, Oroville, CA 95965.

Technical Communication. Society for Technical Communication, 815 15th St. NW, Washington, DC, 20005.

Guides to Technology

Many technical writers find a knowledge of computers, electronics, telephone systems, and data communications helpful in their work since a large portion of the available jobs are in these industries. Good basic guides to these technologies are listed below:

Bell, Paula. *High-Tech Writing: How to Write for the Electronics Industry.* New York: John Wiley & Sons, 1985. Tells how to write instruction manuals. The first two sections tell what goes into each section of a manual. The next two sections cover the writing and revision process.

Balachandran, Sarojini. *Writing: A Bibliography.* Washington, DC: Society for Technical Communications, 1977. A descriptive bibliography listing selected articles and books on technical writing published between 1965 and 1977. Somewhat dated now, but still useful.

Bly, Robert W., and Gary Blake. *Elements of Technical Writing.* New York: MacMillan, 1994. A style guide for technical writers.

Computer Basics: Understanding Computers. Alexandria, VA: Time-Life Books, 1985. A clear, readable, yet comprehensive introduction to computers. Valuable for its thorough definitions of many computer terms commonly used in technical manuals. Useful to writers who write computer manuals.

Noll, A. Michael. *Introduction to Telephones and Telephone Systems.* Norwood, MA: Artech House, Inc., 1986. Nontechnical introduction to telephones, telephone equipment, telephone systems, telecommunications networks, and the jargon that goes with the technology. Useful to writers covering telecommunications-related topics.

Sample Resume

John Doe   Technical Writer
100 Summertown Drive   Industrial Copywriter
Anyplace, USA   Training Specialist
phone 000-0000

TECHNICAL WRITING EXPERIENCE

6/95-present. ACE CHEMICAL COMPANY, *Boonton, New Jersey.*

Polymer mixing manual—produced installation, operation, and maintenance manual for a polymer mixing system used in injection molding operations. I had complete responsibility for the organization, data gathering, and writing of this manual through the printing stage, and I developed illustrations to explain theory of operation, wiring, and parts location. Customers found manual to be interesting, accurate, and easy to follow.

Other technical literature—although I am responsible for writing technical manuals from scratch, I also prepare technical papers, press releases, and product literature. For example, I edited and supervised the production and printing of a technical paper on the performance of motionless mixers.

6/92-9/75. *LIGHTNING ELECTRONICS CORPORATION, Paterson, New Jersey*

Shipboard radar manual—wrote a theory of operation manual on the W-120 shipboard fire control radar system. My responsibilities included setting up production schedule for typing and illustrations through the repro stage.

X-100 radar brochure—wrote and produced a glossy, four color, twelve-page sales brochure on the X-100 air traffic control radar system. Brochure describes capabilities, performance criteria, and operation of this airport surveillance radar.

Product information sheets—wrote product information sheets on the WX-200 modular shipboard fire control system, TCCS air traffic control communications system, X-100-AR air route surveillance radar, and other electronic systems.

ENGINEERING EDUCATION
9/88-5/92. B.S. in chemical engineering, University of Rochester, Rochester, NY

RELATED ACTIVITIES
7/92–present. *Associate member,* American Institute of Chemical Engineers.
3/95–present. *Free-lance writer.* Publication credits include articles in *Science, Books and Films, Baltimore City Paper,* and *The Rochester Patriot.*

REFERENCES AND PORTFOLIO
Will be pleased to submit upon request

CHAPTER NINE

Writing for Television and Film

Careers in Television for Writers

A word repeated over and over by successful television people is sacrifice. You have to be willing to start in a dull job with long hours and low pay—and stick with it awhile—before you can move up. As Barbara Walters explains:

"Whether it's a woman or a man who's getting anywhere, if you are ambitious, you don't give up when the job is grubby and boring. I've had some boring jobs. If you really do want it, you've got to be available to work very long hours—women and men—you have to work longer and harder than anybody else. You have to be available that Saturday. You can't go home at five o'clock, especially in this business. If something comes up and you've got to travel, you've got to be able to do it."

In a survey made a few years back, television executives were asked to identify the primary considerations they took into account when hiring employees. Seven qualifications lead the list: experience, personality, attitude, ability to speak and write clearly, skill in operating station equipment, awareness of the station's relationship with its audience, and the ability to think.

If you're still in school, you might consider tailoring your studies to the television industry. Does your school have a campus television or radio station? Get involved with it as an extracurricular activity. And instead of slinging hash or sitting in a lifeguard's chair this summer, see if you can get an internship with a local station in your hometown or college town.

College isn't a prerequisite to working in television (a high school degree is), but we recommend it to anyone planning to go beyond the lower levels. Nowadays, many people in the higher network positions even have advanced degrees.

Pick the course of study that will best prepare you for your chosen career: English, history, journalism, or communications for television news; business administration for sales or corporate management. Most stations today use computers to manage sales, programming, and promotion, so computer courses can make you more marketable.

More than two hundred colleges and universities offer degrees in television broadcasting. Hundreds of others offer a wide variety of related courses. Check the schools in your area to see what they offer. If you're out of school and already working, a couple of courses at night school may fill in some of the gaps in your knowledge.

The Job Search: Getting Started

The first step in trying to get a job in television is the same as in any other business. You write a resume, print copies, and send them out to potential employers with a cover letter. Then you follow up by phone and mail and hope someone is interested enough to give you an interview.

Unless you're an actor or an on-air personality, don't send your photo with the resume. Don't use fancy borders, colored papers, or oddball designs. The resume should highlight your experience—especially any experience in broadcasting, cable television, audiovisual production, sales, writing, marketing, or any other field related to the job you're seeking.

Use the simplest outline form possible. Avoid long sentences. Don't bore the reader with such meaningless trivia as height, weight, health, or marital status. Include hobbies and extracurricular activities only if they relate to the job at hand. Don't put an objective or goal at the top of the resume. Save the objective for the cover letter, and tailor it to the specific job you want. Stress clerical skills, because if you're a beginner, starting as a secretary may be the best way for you to break in.

The resume should describe your experience while the cover letter persuades the reader to give you an interview. A cover letter is your opportunity to sell yourself to the employer.

Here's a cover letter that was sent to network executives and resulted in interviews for the writer:

THE ONLY PROBLEM WITH WORKING AT THE CUTTING EDGE OF COMMUNICATIONS IS STAYING AHEAD OF THE BLADE.

To stay ahead, you need aggressive people—willing to take chances.

People who are confident, flexible, dedicated.

People who want to learn—who are not afraid to ask questions.

I am one of those people—one of the people you should have on your staff.

Let me prove it. Start by reading my resume. It shows I can take any challenge and succeed.

I want to succeed for you. But if you're looking for someone comfortable with covering the same old ground, count me out.

If you want to work at the cutting edge, call me.

I won't get cut.

The letter was printed on a tasteful gray stock. A picture of a cutting knife was splashed across the top half of the page at a forty-five-degree angle.

This letter is unusual and far from perfect. For one thing, it's too vague, too general. It doesn't say who the writer is, what job he wants, or why the network should hire him.

1

On the other hand, the tone is brash and bold without being offensive. The writer's personality comes through, and he seems a likable, aggressive, self-confident fellow—the kind of guy a network would indeed like to hire. Perhaps that's why this unconventional letter generated results.

Where do you send your letter? To local stations, networks, independent producers, educational stations, cable television ...wherever you want to work.

The best source of names and addresses is *Broadcasting Yearbook*; another good directory is *Television Factbook*. These and other sources of information are described at the end of this chapter. If you're in school or have recently graduated, the campus placement bureau might be able to uncover additional leads.

You can also learn where the jobs are by reading industry trade journals and by attending conferences and seminars. Even if a chance meeting at a reception or luncheon doesn't lead to work, you may make a contact that could pay off sometime in the future.

Be aggressive in your letter-writing campaign. If your response rate is one in twenty, you will get two responses if you send out forty letters, but five responses if you send out a hundred. If you want to be a researcher, writer, or associate producer for a network-produced show (news, feature, or soap), don't go through personnel. Instead, write directly to the executive producer of the show because the producer is the one who decides whom to hire. Personnel merely screens candidates. The producer's name will be listed in the closing credits of the show you're interested in.

If you want to get involved in the production of prime-time entertainment shows, go to the independent production company that produces the show, not the network that broadcasts it. Again, you'll find the production company listed in the closing credits.

When sending any cover letter, take the time to find out the name of the person you want to read it. Address your letter to that specific person. Never use a form letter or a letter that begins with "Dear Television Executive" or "Dear Sir." In job hunting, personalized mail gets the best results.

Follow up by phone as well as by mail. The best time to call a potential employer is during lunch, because the secretary won't be there to pick up the phone and screen your call.

You can also talk to many hard-to-reach people by calling after five in the evening, when the secretary has gone home but the executive is still at work. Executives are often more relaxed after five because the business day is officially over, and this can make them more receptive to your sales pitch.

When employers don't have an opening for you, they'll write back a polite note saying that your resume is being kept on file. This may be true, but it does you no good because no one ever looks at this file. When a job opens up, the resumes that cross the producer's or executive's desk that day are the ones that get read. So be sure to develop a mailing list of key television people and regularly mail your resume to them.

Your persistence will pay off and lead to interviews. The success or failure of the interview depends largely on the personal chemistry between you and the interviewer. "The first thing we look for is a good attitude," says Bruce Whigham, placement manager for CBS. "And during the interview we can tell. We want somebody who makes the company look good."

To Whigham, a good attitude means being willing to make sacrifices. "Somebody who has aspirations but is willing to make sacrifices—that's what gets my attention," says Whigham. He points out that at CBS, "security guards, secretaries, and mailroom people have college educations in communications. They take these positions just to get in the door."

The hard part is getting in. Once you're in, it's easier—although still by no means easy—to move around and up. Insiders have access to those valuable listings of job openings. And the networks prefer to promote from within in many instances.

If a full-time job eludes you, you might try for a spot with ABC's or NBC's vacation-relief programs. From March to October, these two networks hire temporary help to relieve vacationing staffers. The requirements for working vacation relief are less stringent than for full-time employment; a year's experience with a cable or educational station can qualify you to work vacation relief on a network news program or daytime soap opera. Best of all, CBS hires NBC and ABC vacation-relief people for full-time jobs because they have already been trained "free" by the competition.

Whatever the job, don't be afraid to start at the bottom. Take an entry-level position as a clerk or typist. Start at a small station and go on to bigger markets. Work at a job that doesn't thrill you if it gives you a chance to get the job of your dreams. "You don't make jumps from Butte, Montana, to New York," Whigham points out. "You make gradual moves from market to market."

Pay attention to the way your station or network operates—how things are done, who holds the real power, where the jobs are, how new openings are filled. Be aware that no two employers are alike in this industry. NBC does things differently than CBS. WPIX does things differently than WOR. "Every station has career paths—predetermined training and advancement procedures that follow a specific pattern," says Whigham. "You just have to know how they operate."

If you have a chance to step in and help out when there's extra work, do so. It's a good way to get noticed and appreciated. By proving that you are able and willing to handle emergencies and work long hours, you will endear yourself to those who are in a position to promote you.

Television is as difficult to break into as any field in this book, yet you don't need greatly specialized skills or knowledge to succeed. Persistence, ambition, and aggressiveness are at least as important as experience, education, and technical know-how.

And if at first you don't succeed, keep at it, as did Ted Koppel, host of ABC's "Nightline." As Koppel explains: "I couldn't get a job in broadcasting right away.... I looked extraordinarily young, and so people were able to overlook the great potential there. But I knew I was pretty good and would be able to do it. This industry never has been, and I guess never will be, over-populated with brilliance."

Screenwriting

Let's say your dream is to write a screenplay and have it made into a movie. How do you go about it?

First, you need to learn the craft. College courses and how-to books in screenwriting can get you started. The Writer's Guild (555 West Fifty-seventh Street, New York, NY 10019) has some handy publications on screenplay format and screen-writers' fees.

Second, you need to know how to sell your screenplay. Screenplays are bought or contracted for by producers and motion-picture studios. But these people won't read your material unless you're represented by an agent. A complete listing of script agents can be found in *Literary Market Place*, an annual directory published by R. R. Bowker.

How far you want to develop your screenplay before approaching an agent is up to you. A script starts as a *premise*—a one- or two-sentence description that sums up what the film is all about. The premise can be developed into a *treatment*, a fifteen- to twenty-page prose description of the plot of the story. A finished *feature-length film script* will run anywhere from 90 to 120 typewritten pages. If you have contacts in the business, you may be able to sell them the bare bones of an idea over lunch or cocktails. If you're new at the game, write the whole script and sell the complete package.

Aside from college courses and how-to books, there's no formal training available for aspiring screenwriters. The best way to learn is to hunt down some published scripts (many film scripts are published in book form and available at bookstores) and study them. And, of course, you should write and rewrite your own screenplays until you feel they're good enough to sell. Screenwriter Rosemarie Santini says journalism is good training for screenwriting because it teaches you to condense a lot of facts into a tight story.

Most people who dream of selling their scripts never do. But if you succeed at screenwriting, you can earn considerable sums. A large studio will pay upward of $250,000 for a single feature-film script. A few scripts have sold for seven figures. Be aware, though, that just because you sell a script it doesn't guarantee it will be made into a film; many studios buy hundreds of scripts a year but produce only a dozen or so. "Most Hollywood writers make money writing stuff that never goes to camera," Santini laments.

Suggested Reading List in Television

Periodicals

Action. The Directors Guild of America, 1516 Westwood Blvd., Suite 102, Los Angeles, CA 90024. Covers TV and film news relevant to industry professionals.

Back Stage. 165 W. 46th St., New York, NY 10023. Weekly newspaper of the entertainment industry.

Broadcasting. 1735 DeSales St. NW, Washington, DC 20036. Weekly. The bible of the television industry.

Broadcast Engineering, Box 12901, Overland Park, KS 66212. Monthly. For owners, managers, and top technical people at TV stations. Technically oriented articles.

Broadcast Management/Engineering, 295 Madison Ave., New York, NY 10017. Monthly. For broadcast executives, general managers, chief engineers, and program directors of TV stations.

Channels Magazine, Media Commentary Council, Inc., 1515 Broadway, New York, NY 10036. Bimonthly magazine on television and radio communications.

Daily Variety, 1400 N. Cahuenga Blvd., Hollywood, CA 90028. Reports daily on news and events in TV, theater, and film.

Journal of Broadcasting, Broadcast Education Association, 1771 N. St. NW, Washington, D.C. 20036. Quarterly.

Media Decisions, 342 Madison Ave., New York, NY 1001. Monthly. Deals with the advertising side of the television business.

Promotion Newsletter, Radio and TV, Drawer 50108, Lighthouse Point, FL 33064. Monthly newsletter covering the promotional activities of various television and radio stations.

Radio and Television Weekly, 254 E. 31st St., New York, NY 10001. General news and information.

Ross Reports Television, Television Index, 150 Fifth Ave., New York, NY 10011. Detailed information on script and casting requirements of continuing television programs.

Television Digest, 1836 Jefferson Place NW, Washington, DC 20036. Weekly.

Television International Magazine, Box 2430, Hollywood, CA 90028. For management and creative members of the TV industry. Published every two months.

Television Quarterly, National Academy of Television Arts and Sciences, 110 W. 57th St., New York, NY 10019. Quarterly.

Television/Radio Age, Television Editorial Corporation, 666 Fifth Ave., New York, NY 10020. Biweekly.

TV Guide, Radnor, PA 19088. Weekly TV listings plus articles about people and TV shows.

Variety, 154 W. 46th St., New York, NY 10036. Weekly.

Books

Barnouw, Erik. *The Image Empire: A History of Broadcasting in the United States From 1953.* New York: Oxford University Press, 1970. A history of the television industry from 1953 to 1970. Comprehensive but rather heavy reading.

Brooks, Tim, and Earle Marsh. *The Complete Directory to Prime Time Network TV Shows*. New York: Ballantine Books, 1980. An alphabetical guide to every prime-time network show that aired from 1946 to the present. Must-reading for trivia buffs.

Brown, Les. *Television: The Business Behind the Box*. New York: Harcourt Brace Jovanovich, 1971. Highly readable account of the television industry and the networks' competition to be number one in the ratings.

Quinlan, Sterling. *Inside ABC: American Broadcasting Company's Rise to Power*. New York: Hastings House, 1979. A history of ABC. Highly readable, with insights into the minds of top network executives.

Wurtzel, Alan. *Television Production*. New York: McGraw-Hill, 1979. Covers all technical and aesthetic aspects of producing television shows, including editing, special effects, remote operations, and digital equipment.

Directories

Broadcasting Yearbook. Broadcasting Publications, Inc., 1735 DeSales St. NW, Washington, DC 20036. Lists addresses and names of management personnel in TV stations, production companies, and ad agencies.

TV Factbook. 1836 Jefferson Place NW, Washington, DC 20037. Similar in content to *Broadcasting Yearbook*.

Twelve City Directory. Television/Radio Age, 1270 Sixth Ave., New York, NY 10020. Addresses and phone numbers of agencies, networks, TV stations, trade associations, and program syndicators. Contains over six thousand listings.

Organizations of Interest to Television Professionals

Alternate Media Center. 725 Broadway, New York, NY 10003; (212) 260-3990. Internship programs in commercial television.

American Women in Radio and Television. 1321 Connecticut Ave. NW, Washington, D.C. 20036. Association for women in TV and radio.

Announcer Training Studios. 152 W. 42nd St., New York, NY 10036. Training program for TV announcers.

Association of Motion Picture and TV Producers. 8480 Beverly Blvd., Los Angeles, CA 90048. Trade organization of TV and film producers.

Boston Film/Video Foundation. 39 Brighton Ave., Allston, MA 02134.
Provides equipment and information to independent video artists.

Center for Media Arts. 226 W. 26th St., New York, NY 10001. Seminars
and career-placement services in television.

Communications Workers of America. 1925 K St. NW, Washington, DC
20006.

Contract Services Administration Trust Fund. 8480 Beverly Blvd.,
Hollywood, CA 90048. Training programs in television-related fields.

Directors Guild of America. 8480 Beverly Blvd., Hollywood, CA 90048.
Two-year internships with various TV programs.

International Brotherhood of Electrical Workers, Broadcast and Recording Department. 1125 15th St. NW, Washington, DC 20005. Union
representing technicians at CBS and some three hundred to four
hundred independent TV stations throughout the country.

National Academy of Television Arts and Sciences. 110 W. 57th St., New
York, NY 10019. Trade association for television professionals.

National Association of Broadcast Employees and Technicians. 1776
Broadway, Suite 1900, New York, NY 10019. Union representing film
and tape personnel, broadcast technicians, and newswriters.

National Association of Broadcasters. 1771 N St. NW, Washington, DC
20036.

National Association of Educational Broadcasters. 1346 Connecticut
Ave. NW, Washington, DC 20036.

North American Television Institute. 701 Westchester Ave., White
Plains, NY 10604. Seminars in production, technical, and marketing
techniques for the broadcast television industry.

Society of Motion Picture and Television Art Directors. 7715 Sunset
Blvd., Hollywood, CA 90046.

Society of Motion Picture and Television Engineers. 862 Scarsdale Ave.,
Scarsdale, NY 10583. Professional organization dedicated to the
engineering and technical aspects of television.

Television Bureau of Advertising. 485 Lexington Ave., New York, NY
10017.

Television Information Office. 745 Fifth Ave., New York, NY 10022.
Provides informational, promotional, and educational services to the
television industry and to people with an interest in television (writers,
job seekers, and others).

Weist-Barron. 35 W. 45th St., 6th Floor, New York, NY 10036. Courses in
how to audition for a TV commercial.

Women in Communications, Inc. 8305-A Shoal Creek Blvd., Austin, TX
78758. Career counseling for women in broadcasting and other
communications industries.

Writers Guild of America. 22 E. 48th St., New York, NY 10036. Labor
union for TV and film writers.

Young Filmmakers/Video Artists. 4 Rivington St., New York, NY 1000.
Training workshops in TV-studio production for minority youth.

The Big Three: CBS, ABC, NBC

CBS, Inc. 51 W. 52nd St., New York, NY 10019. CBS is a broad-based
   entertainment and communications company. In addition to the
   television network, CBS owns two radio networks, five TV stations,
   thirteen radio stations, a toy company, a musical-instruments company,
   and the world's largest record company, CBS Records. They're also a
   major publisher of books, music, and magazines as well as a producer of
   feature films.

ABC, American Broadcasting Companies. 1330 Sixth Ave., New York,
   NY 10019. ABC describes itself as "a diversified communications,
   entertainment, and information company." Their businesses include
   broadcasting, TV and radio stations, magazine publishing, feature-film
   production, and tourist attractions.

NBC, National Broadcasting Co. 30 Rockefeller Plaza, New York, NY
   10020. RCA owns NBC. RCA also owns Hertz and RCA Records and
   manufactures a variety of products including TV sets, satellites, video
   cassettes, integrated circuits, telex equipment, and defense systems.

Other Major Television Markets

The three major networks have their headquarters in New York
City. But there are TV stations in just about every region of the
country. And starting at a local station is a good way to get
experience and prepare for a career in the big-time.

The twelve major markets in the United States offer opportunities at nearly one hundred good-size stations. Check the
directories listed above for stations in the following cities:

New York	Dallas-Fort Worth
Chicago	St. Louis
Los Angeles	Philadelphia
San Francisco	Minneapolis-St. Paul
Detroit	Boston
Atlanta	Washington, D.C.

TV Training: Where to Find It

Even if you'd rather be an TV anchor, writer, story editor, or producer, a technical understanding of how television broadcasting works is helpful. You should be familiar with the general operation of transmitting and receiving equipment, as well as with federal broadcasting regulations and practices.

Here are some schools that offer technical training in broadcasting:

Ballie School of Broadcast, 2108 E. Thomas Rd., Suite 130, Phoenix, AZ 85016.

Ballie School of Broadcast, 420 Taylor, San Francisco, CA 94102.

Ballie School of Broadcast, 11875 South Bascom, Suite 410, Campbell, CA 95008.

Ballie School of Broadcast, 3045 S. Parker Rd., Suite 223, Building B, Aurora, CO 80014.

Ballie School of Broadcast, 2517 Eastlake Ave. E., Seattle, WA 98102.

Ballie School of Broadcast, The Flour Mill, W. 621 Mallong, Spokane, WA 99201.

Columbia College, 925 N. La Brea Ave., Los Angeles, CA 90038.

Elkins Institute in Dallas, 2603 Inwood Rd., Dallas, TX 79901.

Miller Institute, Main Campus, 4837 E. McDowell Rd., Phoenix, AZ 85008.

Miller Institute, Phoenix Branch Campus, 11062 N. 24th Ave., Phoenix, AZ 85029.

Miller Institute, Spokane Extension Campus, 801 E. Second Ave., Spokane, WA 99202.

National Education Center, Brown Institute Campus, 111 NE 44th St., Fort Lauderdale, FL 33334.

National Education Center, Brown Institute Campus, 3123 E. Lake St., Minneapolis, MN 55403.

Ohio School of Broadcast Technique, 1737 Euclid Ave., Cleveland, OH 44115.

Professional Academy of Broadcasting, 1809 Ailor Ave., Knoxville, TN 37921.

RETS Electronics School, 965 Commonwealth Ave., Boston, MA 02215.

Specs Howard School of Broadcast Arts, 16900 W. Eight Mile Rd., Southfield, MI 48075.

TESST Electronic School, 5122 Baltimore Ave., Hyattsville, MD 20781.

Video Technical Institute, 1806 Royal Lane, Dallas, TX 75229.

Source: Handbook of Trade and Technical Careers and Training: 1984-1985, published by the National Association **of Trade** and Technical Schools (NATTS), Washington, D.C. All schools listed are accredited **by NATTS.**

Required Reading for Future Filmmakers

Periodicals

Action. 1516 Westwood Blvd., Suite 102, Los Angeles, CA 90024. Bimonthly. Covers film news.

The Alpha Viewfinder. Alpha Cine Laboratory, 1001 Lenora St., Seattle, WA 98121. Quarterly. Contains classified help-wanted ads for jobs in the film industry.

American Cinematographer. ASC Holding Corp., 1782 N. Orange Drive, Hollywood, CA 90028. Monthly magazine on film production and cinematography.

American Cinemeditor. 422 South Western Ave., Los Angeles, CA 90020. Quarterly. Articles on film editing.

American Film. American Film Institute, John F. Kennedy Center for the Performing Arts, Washington, DC 20566. Monthly magazine for film professionals, teachers, and enthusiasts.

American Premiere. 183 N. Martel, Suite 1, Los Angeles, CA 90036. Monthly magazine for and about people in the film industry—executives, producers, directors, actors, and others.

Back Stage. 165 W. 46th St., New York, NY 10023. Weekly. Career-related articles and help-wanted ads in film and other entertainment industries.

Boxoffice Magazine. RLD Publishing Corp., 1800 N. Highland Ave., Suite 316, Hollywood, CA 90028. Monthly magazine about the motion-picture industry. Aimed at theater owners, film producers, directors, and financiers.

Cineaste Magazine. 200 Park Ave. S., New York, NY 10003. A quarterly magazine on the art and politics of the cinema. For students enthusiasts, and people who make or distribute films.

Daily Variety. 1400 N. Cahuenga Blvd., Hollywood, CA 90028. Daily newspaper covering the motion-picture and entertainment industry in Hollywood.

Film Comment. Film Society of Lincoln Center, 140 W. 65th St., New York, NY 10023. Bimonthly magazine for film buffs.

Filmmakers Monthly. P.O. Box 115, Ward Hill, MA 08130. Covers feature-film and independent-video production.

Film Quarterly. University of California Press, Berkeley, CA 94720. Quarterly. In-depth analytical articles on the style and structure of films.

The Hollywood Reporter. 6715 Sunset Blvd., Hollywood, CA 90028. Daily. Complete coverage of the entertainment industry, with special focus on the financial aspects of show business.

The Independent. 625 Broadway, New York, NY 10012. Newsletter for independent filmmakers.

Millimeter. 826 Broadway, New York, NY 10003. Monthly. Features articles on the film industry.

Moving Image. Sheptow Publishing Co., 609 Mission St., San Francisco, CA 94105. Published eight times a year. How-to, informational, and technical articles on filmmaking.

On Location Magazine. 6777 Hollywood Blvd., Suite 501, Hollywood, CA 90028. Bimonthly. Covers film and tape production; articles are technically oriented.

Photo Screen. Sterling's Magazines, 355 Lexington Ave., New York, NY 10017. Bimonthly. Articles on movie and TV stars.

ScriptWriter Magazine for Entertainment Writers. 250 W. 57th St., Suite 1432, New York, NY 10019. Monthly magazine for scriptwriters.

Shooting Commericals Magazine. Knowledge Industry Publications, Inc., 701 Westchester, White Plains, NY 10604. Emphasizes commercial production for production companies, ad agencies, equipment houses, and actors.

Show Business. 134 W. 44th St., New York, NY 10036. Weekly. For performers, producers, technicians, directors.

SMPTE Journal. Society of Motion Picture and Television Engineers, 862 Scarsdale Ave., Scarsdale, NY 10583. Monthly technical journal on motion-picture and TV production.

Weekly Variety. 154 W. 46th St., New York, NY 10036. For entertainment professionals.

Directories

Audiovisual Market Place. R. R. Bowker Company, New York, NY 10036. Annual directory listing audiovisual producers, distributors, production companies, and related associations.

Film Daily Year Books. Film Daily, New York, NY. Directory of motion picture companies, services, and personnel.

Guide to Film and Video Resources. University Film Study Center, Cambridge, MA 02138. Lists film-production companies.

International Motion Picture Almanac. Quigley Publishing Company, 159 W. 53rd St., New York, NY 10022. Annual directory of the film industry. Lists producers, distributors, services, agents, organizations, and unions.

On Location: The National Film and Videotape Production Directory. 6777 Hollywood Blvd., Suite 501, Hollywood, CA 90028. Annual directory of film and videotape productionrelated services-production facilities, film processing, insurance, lighting, hotels, truck rentals, casting, etc.

Pacific Coast Studio Directory. Hollywood, CA 90028. Quarterly directory listing production companies, representatives, agents, unions, guilds, organizations, and associations.

Books

Behlmer, Rudy, ed. *Memo from David O. Selznick*. New York: Viking, 1972. A behind-the-scenes look at the making of *Gone with the Wind* and other Selznick classics, as chronicled in Selznick's personal correspondence.

Brownlow, Kevin. *Hollywood: The Pioneers*. New York: Knopf, 1979. Film history illustrated with three hundred rare photographs of early Hollywood.

Capra, Frank. *The Name Above the Title*. New York: Macmillan, 1971. Capra's autobiography.

Kael, Pauline. *Deeper Into Movies*. Boston: Little, Brown, 1973. A collection of movie reviews from one of the best-respected movie critics in the country. Useful for its insight into the role movies play in American culture.

Kanin, Garson. *Hollywood*. New York: Viking, 1974. Autobiographical account of Hollywood in the 1930s and 1940s by one of its most celebrated writer-directors.

Mast, Gerald. *A Short History of the Movies*. New York: Bobbs-Merrill, 1971. Traces the evolution of the motion-picture industry from 1895 to 1970.

Pechter, William S. *Twenty-four Times a Second: Film and FilmMakers*. New York: Harper & Row, 1971. A collection of critical essays on film, filmmakers, and the theory of film appreciation.

Robertson, Joseph F. *The Magic of Film Editing*. New York: Television/Radio Age Books. Covers every aspect of professional film editing from script to screen.

Shurtleff, Michael. *Audition: Everything an Actor Needs to Know to Get the Part*. New York: Bantam Books, 1978. How to audition successfully for stage and screen.

Professional Societies and Other Organizations of Interest to Film Professionals

American Film Institute Academy, Center for Advance Film Studies. 501 Doheny Rd., Beverly Hills, CA 90210. Internship program in feature-film production.

Artists Managers Guild. 9255 Sunset Blvd., Suite 930, Los Angeles, CA 90069. Guild for Hollywood agents and managers.

Association of Independent Video and Filmmakers. 625 Broadway, New York, NY 10012. Support services for independent filmmakers.

Association of Motion Picture and TV Producers. 8480 Beverly Blvd., Los Angeles, CA 90048. A trade association representing producers and studios.

Astoria Motion Picture and Television Center Foundation. 35-11 35th Ave., Astoria, NY 11106. Internship program in film.

Boston Film/Video Foundation. 39 Brighton Ave., Allston, MA 02134. Provides equipment and information to independent filmmakers.

Career Planning Center. 1623 South La Cienega Blvd., Los Angeles, CA 90035. Offers a seminar in careers in the film industry.

Contract Services Administration Trust Fund. 8480 Beverly Blvd., Hollywood, CA 90048. Training programs in film-related fields.

Directors Guild of America. 8480 Beverly Blvd., Hollywood, CA 90048. Training program for directors.

Directors Guild of America. 1697 Broadway, Suite 405, New York, NY 10019. Training program for film producers.

The Film Fund. 80 E. 11th St., Suite 647, New York, NY 10003. Gives grants to producers of documentary and dramatic films.

Good People. 827 Hilldale Ave., Los Angeles, CA 90069. Employment agency specializing in show business.

Institute of New Cinema Artists. 505 Eighth Ave., New York, NY 10001. Training programs in technical areas of film and television for disadvantaged youth.

International Alliance of Theatrical Stage Employees and Moving Picture Machine Operators (IATSE). Local 659, 8480 Beverly Blvd., Hollywood, CA 90048. Training program for film camera operators and special-effects assistants.

Motion Picture Association of America. 522 Fifth Ave., New York, NY 10036. Trade association for large motion-picture production companies and distributors.

National Association of Broadcast Employees and Technicians (NABET). 135 W. 50th St., New York, NY 10022.Union for movie and TV engineers and technicians.

Neighborhood Film Project. 3601 Locust Walk, Philadelphia, PA 19104. Filmmaking workshops.

New School for Social Research. 66 W. 12th St., New York, NY 10011. Courses in filmmaking.

New York Foundation for the Arts. 5 Beekman St., Suite 600, New York, NY 10038. Placement program for artists in film.

New York University, Department of Cinema Studies. School of the Arts, 51 W. Fourth St., New York, NY 10003. Degree programs in cinema studies.

Northwest Film Study Center. Portland Art Museum, 1219 S.W. Park Ave., Portland, OR 97205. Internships and courses in filmmaking.

Screen Publicists Guild. 13 Astor Pl., New York, NY 10003. Guild of film publicists.

Sherwood Oaks Experimental College., 6353 Hollywood Blvd., Hollywood, CA 90028. Programs in filmmaking.

Society of Motion Picture and Television Engineers. 862 Scarsdale Ave. Scarsdale, NY 10583. Professional organzation for film engineers and technicians.

University of California, Theater Arts Department. 405 Helgard Ave., Los Angeles, CA 90024. Degree programs in film production, scriptwriting, and criticism.

University of Southern California, Division of Cinema. School of Performing Arts, University Park, Los Angeles, CA 90007. Academic program leading to a career as a film executive or independent producer.

Women of the Motion Picture Industry. International, c/o HOWCO International, P.O. Box 1805, Charlotte, NC 28201. Publishes a newsletter for women in the movie business. Also offers career counseling.

Women's Interart Center. 549 W. 52nd St., New York, NY 10019. Workshops in filmmaking.

Writers Guild of America. 8955 Beverly Blvd., Los Angeles, CA 90048. Labor union for film scriptwriters.

Writers Guild of America. 555 W. 57th St., New York, NY 10022.

Young FilmmakerslVideo Arts. 4 Rivington St., New York, NY 10002. Film workshops.

Free-Lancing

The Self-Employment Option

Some careers offer more opportunity for self-employment than other professions. Writing is one of them. Others include typing, word processing, graphic design, accounting, medicine, computer programming, interior design, and law.

Other careers and occupations have limited opportunity for self-employment and usually require you to work for an organization. These include chemistry, investment banking, purchasing, marine biology, art history, teaching English, and managing.

Most writers consider self-employment at some point in their careers. Some treat it as a new career. For others, it's a way to generate revenue between full-time jobs. Or after hours.

What about you? Does free-lancing beckon? Before you make the transition from corporate to self-employment, consider the pros and cons carefully.

Pros and Cons of Free-Lancing

There are many advantages to being self-employed. These include the freedom to:

- work at home

- live in whatever part of the country you want to

- dress in casual clothes

- sleep late

- keep nonstandard office hours

- work when you feel like it

- take vacation whenever you want to

- do what you want, when you want

- take as many sick days or personal days as you need

- do projects you enjoy

- reject projects that don't interest you

- refuse to work with people you don't like

- be your own boss

- enjoy tax deductions others don't

- occasionally make a lot of money on certain projects

- eat when you want to

- exercise or shop during the middle of the day, when health clubs and stores are less crowded

- have the radio, TV, or stereo on all day, if you wish

- build a considerable portfolio of writing samples

- avoid office politics

- avoid commuting

- minimize boring and unnecessary meetings

- minimize paperwork and administrative tasks

- avoid having a boss or employees to deal with

- avoid golf outings, family day, and other corporate events that infringe on your personal time

- get paid for all the hours you work for your clients

- not be ruled by the dictates of a boss or corporate culture

- spend less money on transportation, clothing, and dry cleaning

- spend more time with your family

There are also disadvantages. As a free-lancer, you:

- don't receive a regular pay check

- have uneven cash flow

- may not qualify for mortgages or other loans in amounts you would qualify for if you had a full-time job

- have to constantly market and sell yourself

- have to constantly negotiate fees, advances, and royalties

- give 10 to 15 percent of your earnings to any agents or sales reps who represent you

- don't get benefits such as health insurance or expense accounts

- pay for office space, equipment, and supplies out of your own pocket

- pay for private health insurance

- have to please a variety of clients with different tastes and requirements

- have to travel to visit some clients at their offices

- attend many sales meetings, without compensation, that result in no sale or assignment

- deal with slow-paying clients and some clients who don't pay

- finance your retirement plan out of your earnings with no matching contributions from employers

- deal with clients who want to change what you write or don't listen to your advice

- motivate yourself to work when no one is telling you to

- cope with isolation and loneliness

- pay the salary of a secretary or typing service when you need these services

- explain to unbelieving friends and relatives that when you are home, you are working much of the time

- work whatever hours are required to meet your deadlines

- make yourself work when you don't feel like working

- juggle the demands of multiple clients, assignments, and priorities

- keep up with computer technology and learn the latest software

- get involved with nonwriting aspects of running a free-lance business, such as bookkeeping and taxes

When to Go Free-Lance

Is there a best time to try free-lancing? Maybe. But if you wait for the "perfect time" to free-lance, you may reach retirement before you ever do it.

When it comes to making the transition from corporate employment to self-employment, there is always a reason to delay: an upcoming raise, a Christmas bonus, a promotion due you, or a current assignment you want to finish.

It will never be the ideal time to quit your job and give up your comfortable office, salary, and benefits. For this reason, many writers who dream of making the transition from staff to free-lance never do. And this is perfectly okay.

The free-lance life is exciting, but also uncertain. You do not have the comfort and security of knowing for certain that you will make X amount of money this week or this month. On a small scale, free-lancers are risk takers, trading the certainty of a paycheck for the uncertainty of free-lance work.

Free-lancers may have no allegiance to an employer, but there is no employer with an allegiance to you, the freelancer—just clients who hire you on a project-by-project basis. In fact, the term "free lance" comes from the Middle Ages; it was used to describe warriors who had no allegiance to any monarchy but would work as mercenaries for whichever kingdom would pay their fee.

An ideal time to try free-lancing is when you have been laid off or fired from one job. Instead of getting another full-time job, why not try free-lancing? Free-lancing can pay some bills and keep you busy until you find another job. And, if the free-lancing goes really well, you can continue with it and stop searching for a conventional job.

Other than being the victim of corporate restructuring or downsizing, there is no ideal time to go free-lance. A lot depends on your tolerance for risk and your income requirements.

When I went free-lance in February, 1982, I had very little money, but also very few expenses or responsibilities: I lived in a one-room apartment, didn't have a family to support, and didn't own a car. I was only twenty-four years old, with no one dependent on me.

Today, I am in my late thirties, and my financial obligations are more considerable: I support a wife and two young children; I pay a mortgage on a house, have two cars, and must save not only for my retirement but for college for my two children, an expense that will probably exceed $350,000. I must also, through costly life and disability insurance, provide for my family should I die or become disabled.

I often wonder if I would make the leap from corporate employment to free-lance employment today as readily and easily as I did in 1982. I think I would not: I am not a risk taker, and I would be afraid of losing the security and income of a corporate job. What about you?

Ultimately your decisions as to whether and when to try free-lancing are driven by an examination of the risks and rewards. You balance the benefits and perks of the job you have now with the greater potential income and freedom of free-lancing. You weigh how afraid you are to quit your job against how dissatisfied you are with it.

One useful technique is to divide a piece of paper into two columns. Label the paper "Pros and Cons of Free-Lancing." Label the left column "Cons" and the right column "Pros." In the two columns, list the reasons to stay in your job versus the reasons to quit and try free-lance writing. Whichever column has more persuasive arguments in it determines your decision.

Do not feel, as I did, that if you quit the corporate world to try free-lancing, you will somehow "damage" the perfect track record of employment on your resume and therefore become unhirable. When I worked in corporate America in the late 1970s, a perfect chronological resume was expected, and employment gaps were cause for alarm. Today, with frequent downsizing affecting thousands of workers monthly, there is no longer a stigma attached to having a gap in your resume between corporate positions. So that particular risk element of trying free-lancing has been eliminated.

Getting Started

I assume you now work for an organization. The question is: How do you make the transition from corporate employment to self-employment?

Here are some initial steps to take:

MOONLIGHT. If you can get away with it, do some free-lance writing on the side. This will give you a feel for free-lancing as you build a portfolio of samples and earn spare-time income. Don't moonlight so much that you put yourself in jeopardy of losing your day job.

SET UP A WRITING OFFICE. Most writers work from home. It's a good idea to set up your home writing office before you go free-lance. That way, all equipment and systems will be in place, and you won't feel overwhelmed at the beginning.

BUY SOME EQUIPMENT. If you can afford it, buy the software, fax machine, modem, printer, or computer you need while you still have a regular income. But if you have quit your job, and cash flow is uncertain, you may be hesitant to spend the money.

This equipment will maximize your productivity and earnings. While writers can get by with minimal office equipment, having modern equipment increases productivity. I regret the way I resisted new technologies (modems, faxes, Internet connections), and would have made more money had I embraced them sooner.

CHOOSE A COMPANY NAME. This is the name under which you will do business. For free-lance writers, I recommend simply using your own name, e.g., "Carol Jones/Writer-Editor." Some writers use corporate-sounding names such as Word Smart Communications or PCM Editorial Services. Others add "& Associates" to their name in attempt to convey the image of a firm rather than an individual. I find this unnecessary.

OPEN A BUSINESS CHECKING ACCOUNT. Business funds should be kept separate from personal funds. To open a business account, you will need to file a certificate of doing business with your local municipality. The forms can be purchased in a stationery or office supply store. Submit three forms for approval—one to keep on file at city hall, one for your bank, and one for your files.

GET YOUR BUSINESS CARDS PRINTED. Also have envelopes and letterhead printed. Start with 500 copies of each. Stationery can be simple—your name, address, phone, and fax number.

Underneath your name, put a simple description of what you do. Possibilities include: free-lance writer, writing services, writing and editorial services, writer/consultant.

Creating a Business Plan

Most writers have no idea how much effort they must exert to earn a given amount of money. Many do not even have an income goal. If you don't know how much you want to make, or what you have to do to make it, you'll have a difficult time financially.

Here's how to create a simple plan for your free-lance writing business:

1. Determine the amount of money you want to earn this year. I'm amazed at how many free-lancers have no financial goal. If you don't know how much money you want to earn, how do you know how much work you have to do, and what you must charge, to make the living you want to make? The average free-lance writer in the United States doing editorial or literary writing earns about $25,000 annually. According to the Cam Foote, publisher of the newsletter *Creative Business,* the average advertising and corporate free-lance writer earns $50,000. I would think setting an income objective for your first year of $25,000 to $50,000 is reasonable.

2. Determine how much you must make to reach your annual income goal. If your goal is $50,000 a year, and you work 50 weeks a year, you must make $1,000 a week, $200 a day, $4,167 per month. Knowing what you must earn each day, week, or month tells you whether you are on track to make your goal.

3. Determine your average project fee. Project fees will vary, of course, but how much will you earn for each project on

average? If your average fee per article is $1,000, you must write and sell one article or pamphlet per week to achieve your $50,000 income goal.

4. Determine the level of sales and marketing activity needed to make your sales goal. If you must write and sell one article a week, and your sales closing rate is one assignment for every five query letters, then you must write and send out five query letters a week, or 250 queries a year.

Only when you have worked out these numbers for your own free-lance business will you have a realistic idea of the effort required to earn a living as a free-lance writer.

Types of Assignments

Free-lance writers handle many different types of assignments. You can write articles for newspapers, magazines, and newsletters under your own by-line. You can write screen plays and scripts for movies and television. Free-lance writers also produce and sell essays, short stories, poems, plays, novels, and nonfiction books.

Publishing is just one of many industries that uses free-lance writers. Most industries do. Staff and free-lance writers handle assignments in banking, pulp and paper, cosmetics, fashion, travel, chemicals, metals, telecommunications, and computers, to name just a few areas. There are dozens more. One writer I know specializes in writing about collectibles (e.g., the porcelain Elvis doll and Franklin Mint Civil War chess set); another writes only about nuclear medicine; a third focuses on the interactive video industry.

Writers are needed to produce everything from annual reports and advertising copy to press releases, proposals, sales letters, and software manuals. There are dozens of other assignments. They include booklets, pamphlets, brochures, catalogs, invoice stuffers, posters, training programs, employee handbooks, and company newsletters.

You can take on the types of assignments that interest you most or that pay the best. Or you can do what comes your way. Some free-lance writers do a combination of both. Even if you pursue one market or area of specialization, other opportunities will come your way, and you have to decide whether to take them on or turn them down.

Specialist or Generalist?

"Should I be a specialist in a particular industry or type of writing, or should I be a generalist, handling what comes my way?"

This is a common question among beginning free-lancers. The answer—that you can do *both* and that they are not mutually exclusive—surprises most.

Richard Armstrong, a Washington, D.C., free-lance writer, has three specialties: speech writing, circulation promotion, and direct-mail fund-raising. But he also writes press releases, articles, ads, and other materials for clients.

Remember my writer friend who specialized in nuclear medicine? She has also handled assignments in diverse topics ranging from fine arts forgeries to political campaign literature.

You can specialize in one, two, or more areas, but also handle general assignments at the same time. Why not? It works!

If you start as a generalist, you will notice that you begin to build experience in various specialties. Embrace those that interest you, and begin pursuing more assignments in these areas.

Every free-lance writer, in addition to being a generalist, should have at least one or two specialty areas. Writers specialize either by subject matter (gardening, science, computers, careers, banking) or by type of assignment (direct mail, annual reports, public relations, manuals).

Why specialize? Specialists have an easier time getting assignments. All else being equal, the client or editor will hire the experienced writer over writers who don't know the topic or format. Specialists generally command higher fees and face less competition. One study in *Adweek* magazine, for example, showed copywriters specializing in high-tech earned $10,000 a year more than those who did general advertising.

Selling Your Services

Numerous free-lance writers make their living writing articles for newspapers and magazines. Some of these writers also turn out books for publishers.

In selling to this type of market, you must come up with ideas for "products" (books and articles), write an outline or proposal for the article or book you want to write, and find a publisher who will pay you to do it. You are selling ideas first and yourself second. The basic tools for selling writing in this manner—query letters, outlines, proposals—are discussed in chapters 2 through 4 of this book on book, magazine, and newspaper writing.

Many free-lance writers focus primarily on business, corporate, and technical writing, selling their writing services to ad agencies, PR firms, small businesses, and corporations. In selling to this type of market, you do not come up with ideas for marketing campaigns or ads and try to find a sponsor for them, as in free-lancing for magazine or book publishers.

Instead, you send out promotional materials offering your services as a writer for hire to potential clients. You are selling yourself and your expertise, and nothing else. Clients, if they decide to hire you, will tell you what the assignment is and what they want you to write. If by chance they do want ideas from you, they will pay you a consulting fee to generate these ideas; corporate clients don't expect you to sit around and propose ideas for free, as magazine editors and book publishers do.

Where do you find potential clients and publishers? Each chapter of this book dealing with a different specialized area (advertising, book publishing, magazines) gives at least one reference you can turn to for lists—including names, addresses, and phone numbers—of potential clients and employers. Contact them with a phone call or by letter. Give editors ideas that fit their publications, and stress to corporate clients how your capabilities meet their needs.

For detailed information on marketing yourself as a freelance writer, send for a free copy of *The Writer's Profit Catalog*. See also my books *Selling Your Services* and *Secrets of a Freelance Writer: How to Make $85,000 a Year*.

Negotiating Your Fee

How much do you charge? How do you negotiate a higher fee or respond if the prospect says "Your price is too high"?

In editorial work—writing for book and magazine publishers—the editor will usually make you an offer. You can accept the offer as presented or ask for more money. It's up to you.

If you are writing books, you can get a literary agent to represent you. The agent will handle all fee negotiations with the publisher, freeing you from this unpleasant and sometimes awkward task.

When writing articles, you can always ask for more money. But are you prepared to turn down the job if the editor won't pay more? If not, accept what they offer until you are in a position—financial and psychological—where you are willing to walk away if they don't meet your price.

For business assignments, clients will ask *you* what it costs. Ask the client if she has a budget or at least a dollar figure in mind. This will enable you to determine whether you can offer a price that meets her range.

Another strategy is to ask other free-lancers what they charge for similar work; many will share this information with you. You also learn what to charge by going to meetings and quoting prices when you have no idea what to charge, then seeing how prospects react. You rapidly learn what is considered too low, too high, and acceptable for a particular type of project.

When you and the client agree on a fee and deadline date, get it in writing. Magazines and book publishers will send contracts. Corporate clients may send purchase orders or ask you to confirm the fee, deadline, and terms in a simple letter of agreement. Write up such a letter and get their signatures on it.

Handling Problems

Writers, as a rule, are introverted people who dislike confrontation. Therefore, they get upset when problems with editors, publishers, or clients occur.

Unfortunately, problems will occur. There is no business that is problem-free, including free-lance writing. If there were, most people would probably be doing it!

The key to handling problems is to avoid geting upset or taking things personally. Writing—and the evaluation of a piece of writing—is highly subjective. At times, what you give the client will not be what he or she expected. Some clients get upset at this, especially if you are working on a tight deadline. When they complain or criticize, it's not to hurt your feelings or to be difficult. They're just concerned about whether you understand the problem they've presented and what they are looking for.

Also, many people in business today are more time-pressured than in years past. This forces them to be quick and abrupt in many of their dealings, to the point of what may seem like rudeness. If someone is short with you, remember he or she may be under a lot of pressure from someone else on this project and isn't deliberately trying to give you a difficult time.

You don't have to agree with the clients or editors who criticizes your work; you merely have to acknowledge that you heard and understood their point of view. If a client says, "This isn't clear to me," don't argue that it is clearly written. But don't agree that it's unclear if you think it's not. Instead, find out what the client thinks is unclear and what points need to be added for clarification.

The biggest mistake free-lance writers make is to be a prima donna. Client satisfaction depends as much (or more) on how you treat the client as on how good your writing is. Clients do not want to deal with writers who are difficult, fussy, argumentative, or who get angry when asked to do revisions. Be pleasant, understanding, and professional at all times—even when you disagree with the client. This is one of the keys to free-lance success.

Expanding Your Free-Lance Business

The single greatest problem for free-lance writers, as well as others offering professional services of all kinds, is the limitation of time. There are only so many hours in the week you can work. Once all that time is taken up with writing projects, you can't take on any more work until these jobs are done. Therefore, free-lance writers frequently are offered more business than they can handle, and as a result, are forced to turn away many lucrative assignments.

One solution is to subcontract some of the work to other freelancers. Writers who subcontract to other writers report they generally give the subcontractor 50 to 80 percent of the project fee, keeping 20 to 50 percent as their compensation for getting the work, assigning it, supervising, editing, and dealing with the client.

Another solution is to go beyond being a solo practitioner and form a small writing firm, ad agency, or PR firm. You can have a partner or hire employees.

I know several writers who formed agencies of this type and increased their incomes by having other writers work for them. The pro is that you can potentially earn more money; the con is the headache of having a company and managing and motivating employees. I have chosen to remain solo, but I often have doubts about the choice I've made (inertia and laziness prevent me from doing much more than worrying about it).

The Two Best Sources of New Business

Free-lance writers tend to get excited when they get a call from a potential new client or a publisher they have never written for. That's understandable: The new is usually more exciting than the old. But, while you will need a steady stream of new clients to keep you busy, the most profitable business is repeat assignments from existing clients.

The tendency is to focus on getting new clients. But don't ignore your current and past clients as a source of lucrative business. Send them a quarterly newsletter or postcard mailing. Clip and mail articles of interest—either your own work or other items. Pick up the phone and call every couple of months. Send your new book or samples of your latest manuals.

"Is this necessary?" you may be asking. "After all, they already have my phone number and they know me. If they need me, they'll call."

Sometimes, yes. But the fact is, clients and editors deal with many writers. Every week, they get promotions and proposals from new writers saying, "Hire me." The writer they have heard from recently may get the assignment instead of you, simply because that writer's name is foremost in the editor's mind. To compete, you periodically have to remind your clients and editors of your existence, so when they think of a writer for a new project, they think of you first.

The second most profitable source of business is referrals: having a satisfied client give your name to colleagues who are potential clients for your writing services.

There is an art to getting referrals. Entire sales training programs and seminars have been presented on this topic, so I cannot adequately cover it here. The key to getting referrals is doing excellent work: Only satisfied clients will give you refer-rals to other potential clients. Do your best for every client, meet your deadlines, be pleasant and agreeable to work with, and charge what you said you would charge. This in itself will lead to many referrals.

Selling Your Writing via Mail Order

There are three basic methods of making money as a free-lance writer:

1. *Write your own words and sell them to publishers.* As we've discussed, you can get contracts to write books for publish-ers or articles for newspapers and magazine editors.

2. *Write other people's words.* This encompasses all forms of corporate and commercial free-lance work, where you write copy on assignment for a client. Assignments range from ghostwriting speeches for busy executives to writing bro-chure and catalog copy.

3. *Write your own words and sell them directly to the consumer.* This option encompasses all forms of mail- order market-ing and self-publishing. You write what you want to write, then pay to have it duplicated as a book, pamphlet, report, video or audio tape, disk, CD-ROM, or some other me-dium. You sell copies directly to readers through a variety of methods, typically via mail order.

Many writers swear by self-publishing. However, many oth-ers swear at it. For each self-publishing success story, where someone published his or her own book and got rich when it became a best-seller, there are dozens with carton upon carton of unsold books gathering dust in their garage or spare bedroom.

The reason is that, while these writers may know how to write, they may not have the time, knowledge, skills, or temperament required to market books and other mail order information products. Anyone can write a manuscript and pay a printer to typeset it and print it in book form. It is quite another thing to know how to market the book and sell thousands of copies while making a profit.

When you study the mail-order book ads and dream of making a similar killing, keep in mind that nine out of ten mail order products fail to make money. Most break even or lose money for the entrepreneur. Ads and direct mailings can be expensive. Often, a self-publisher will invest thousands in a space ad or mailer and not recover a fraction of the cost in sales. It happens all the time.

Writing and selling information products by mail is such a complex and vast subject that I cannot adequately cover it here. I have written a book on mail order selling, called *How to Start and Run a Profitable Mail Order Business*, available from Self-Counsel Press. Many other useful books have been written on this topic, including Dan Poynter's *The Self-Publishing Manual* (Para Publishing).

For most free-lance writers, I recommend self-publishing and mail-order selling as a supplementary source of income. It is quite possible to earn an extra $1,000 to $5,000 a month or more selling your writings direct via mail order, starting with only a small investment.

You might do better, and even get rich, but think of this as a long-term goal, not an immediate or even likely result. Most big mail-order information entrepreneurs are well capitalized.

When should you self-publish versus selling your work to a traditional publisher? Let's look at some guidelines:

- Information, especially how-to, technical, and reference, sells well via mail order. If your writing is mainly informative, self-publishing might be for you. If your writing is mainly entertaining, you're probably better off selling to magazine editors and book publishers.

- Direct marketing is especially effective selling to niche or vertical markets. Therefore, you might consider placing broad, general works with traditional publishers, and self-marketing information aimed at small niche markets.

- A book on "How to Get the Job You Want" would sell well in bookstores and probably should be aimed at a regular publisher. A book on "Getting into Training: A Lucrative Career Option for Teachers" would be too narrow for a mainstream publisher but could be sold via mail order through ads in teacher magazines.

- Products sold via mail order must offer a powerful benefit, excite the audience, and contain information readers perceive they cannot get elsewhere. Hot topics include money, success, relationships, sex, and starting a business. Esoteric, literary, and academic subjects do not normally sell well via mail-order ads or mailings.

- Some writers are more obsessed with the writing and printing of their words than with the selling. If that's you, leave the distribution and sales to a traditional publisher. I know too many writers who, addicted to self-publishing, deplete their savings accounts publishing book after book. They are thrilled when they receive the books from the printers, and that's when their interest ends. They start writing the next book, and the previous books never sell.

  My approach is always to try to sell my writing to a magazine editor or book publisher first. I only consider self-publishing when a traditional publisher is not interested in the work.

- Self-publishing is a viable option for works that are too long for a magazine article, but too short to fill a regular book. These manuscripts would range in length from four thousand to forty thousand words. Such works can be inexpensively self-published in a variety of formats including booklets, special reports, manuals, and audio cassettes.

For instance, a few years ago I self-published a five thousand-word article, "Recession-Proof Business Strategies," as a sixteen-page booklet. The booklets cost thirty-nine cents apiece to print in quantities of one thousand. I charged seven dollars each and sold more than thirty-five hundred at that price. Promotion was mainly via press releases announcing publication of the booklet.

To Sum Up...

Free-lancing. Many writers dream of the free-lance life: working at home in old clothes and slippers; no commuting; peace and tranquillity; freedom from office politics and hassles.

There is, of course, a flip side. Free-lancers get no sick days, no benefits, no pension, no steady paycheck, no paid vacation. They must provide for their own retirement funds, office equipment, office space, supplies, and insurance.

What do I recommend for you? If free-lancing sounds appealing, why not give it a try? If you don't like it, or things don't work out, there are many other career options for writers, as outlined in the previous chapters. Writing is a skill for which there is ongoing, continual demand. Staff or free-lance, you can make a decent living in a writing career.

Often the writing job we dreamed of turns out to be anything *but* a dream job. Many writers start in one area then switch to another because of convenience or the need for greater income. Then, lo and behold, they discover their true calling in this new form of writing! Be open to the twists and turns your career holds in store for you. Writers rarely follow a straight and narrow path. There are more curves and bumps on the road to writing success than in other fields. But the ride can be exciting. Good luck!